We all strive to be.

(Something)

We all trust to believe.

(Someone)

And we all mourn.

The Cruelty of the Classical Canon

Preface

We Libidinal Economists! Daybreak, Version √2

With this debut volume of Zētēsis, the artists, philosophers, designers, technicians and scientists involved with this project and committed to an 'old fashioned' kind of research ~ that which is generated by a curiosity and deep commitment to know (the whatever) ~ declare a new *Daybreak*. It is one that intends to take as a given, complexity and the irrational / imaginary in art and the sciences, physics and metaphysics, culture and its economies, skin and the pleasures of the flesh. It steps to the atonal rhythms of the mimetic patterns of camouflage and the flâneur. It aligns itself with the history of those who were (and remain) willing to ask and act upon this basic question: Supposing it could be otherwise, what would this otherwise look like, become, be, now? We want to say that however it would look, be, become (now), the journey to find out must be fuelled by experiment, rigour, and a willingness to risk.

We owe a strong debt of thanks to our past and present-day interlocutors, from the genealogists, libidinal economists, feminists and queer theory / practitioners to those dancing in, on, and with this new field of 'wild science' and its very welcome co-collaborator, the sensual. We also owe a strong debt of thanks to those who were and remain willing to take a (financial) punt on this possibly awkward, possibly bruised, blue-sky thinking endeavour: The Birmingham School of Art in particular and its wider platform, The Birmingham Institute for Art and Design at BCU along with the staff and student artists, designers, philosophers, technicians, web aficionados, research fellows and scientists who gave generously of their time, despite wider pressures cascading onto their already overworked work schedules.

This is not a perfunctory acknowledgment to the School of Art at BIAD-BCU. For the academic, dare we say, *intellectual* world ~ and the universities that nourish its diversity, strident intelligence, playfulness and rigour ~ seems to have lost its way. This world, our world, challenged as it has been for the last decade or so with profound cuts in the arts & humanities, alongside a gluttonous appetite for all things STEM (Science, Technology, Engineering, Maths), and topped with a seemingly wilful misreading of what constitutes experimentation, thinking, practice, indeed research itself, especially when it comes to art, philosophy, social science, culture, needs a bit of TLC (Tender Loving Care).

So the journal and its future offspring, comes with a warning: be prepared to *think* outside the proverbial box, and to do so, *slowly* and with *care*, as if approaching an untamed but curious beast. As an *aid memoire*, we dedicate this, the first volume, no. 1 to questioning *The Cruelty of the Classical Canon*. Each intervention / contribution / design decision has been peer-reviewed with members from an internationally and discipline-diverse advisory board. Some of the selected pieces support the classical canon; others reject it outright; still others try to strike a delicate balance between outright rejection and the appeal of its tried and tested repertoire. All have something to do with Nietzsche's seminal text, *Daybreak,* Lyotard's shout (demand), *We Libidinal Economists!* and the first discovered imaginary number, √2.[1] It is up to you to decide which is which, and why.

Welcome to Zētēsis: Research Generated by Curiosity.

Johnny Golding
Editor

---

1. Friedrich Nietzsche, *Daybreak: Thoughts on the Prejudices of Morality* (Cambridge Texts in the History of Philosophy), edited by Maudemarie Clark and Brian Leiter, (Cambridge: Cambridge University Press, 2003). Of particular interest, see Nietzsche's remark: "We have to *learn to think differently* ~ in order at last, perhaps very late on, to attain even more: *to feel differently.*" (103). As for libidinal economists, see Jean François Lyotard, *Libidinal Economy,* (London: Continuum, 2004), especially this remark in the chapter, '*The Great Ephemeral Skin*': "I see you, Unkind One, smiling at the hoax played on me by the words of knowledge and capital, before I had even begun to speak. Let us love this farce, let us not fear it, let us say yes each time it *requires* us to (and it will require us to, and require us again) say what we have to say as libidinal economists... (16). And finally, the lovely mad imaginary number , one of the first or perhaps even the first of its kind, discovered on a Babylonian tablet approximately 1800-1600 BC (YBC 7289). Like the Siren's song of Ulysses, it sweeps anyone who tries to uncover its rationality into a torrent of proofs that can only prove (if it proves anything at all) its irrationality. But see in particular, David Flannery, *The Square Root of 2: A Dialogue Concerning a Number and a Sequence,* (New York: Springer: 2010).

The Paradoxical Economy of Crisis:

"Crisis of Experience" and the Ana-Economy of Else

Abstract: Representation is a canon as classic as it is cruel. Within a wider question about the logic of emergence of meaning, it seems very interesting to look at sense not as an a priori but as an aesthetic space (or event), where a distribution of the sensible does not happen without a simultaneous articulation of epistemological categories, and vice-versa. The article concentrates on this reciprocity, or inter-causality, to attempt a critique of the paradigm of representation drawing on Walter Benjamin's work on technology and on Thomas Kuhn's discussion of 'scientific revolutions', in order to analyse how moments of change reveal a 'crisis' where the shortcoming of the economy of such paradigm in engaging with the world become evident. This interdisciplinary approach merges questions from aesthetic and epistemological enquiries through the notion of emergence and feedback loop elaborated by complexity theory.

Representation is a canon as classic as it is cruel. A critique of this paradigm can be attempted by drawing on Walter Benjamin's work on technology and on Thomas Kuhn's discussion of 'scientific revolutions', in order to analyse how moments of change reveal a 'crisis' where the shortcomings of such a paradigm in engaging with the world become evident. This interdisciplinary approach merges questions from aesthetic and epistemological enquiries through the notion of *emergence* and *feedback loop* elaborated by complexity theory, proposing that the possibility of 'making sense', or establishing an economy, rests on a generative logic rather than the representation of an apriori meaning, and requires a reversal of temporality. Indeed the notion of crisis is directly linked to the paradigm of representation. Crises are not exceptional states, rather moments when incommensurable series, or discourses, converge and diverge simultaneously; they are paradoxical economies that escape a 'restricted' model and at the same time do not quite reflect a 'general' economy. In fact crises escape deterministic necessity entirely, they are 'open states' where there is simultaneously less, more, and *else* than what was expected in terms of value as well as meaning.

Within a wider question about the logic of emergence of meaning, it seems very interesting to look at sense as an *aesthetic* space (or event) where a distribution of the sensible does not happen without a simultaneous articulation of epistemological categories, and vice versa. The argument concentrates on this reciprocity, or inter-causality, moving from the extinction of determinism brought about by complexity theory, and introducing a *poietic* form of temporality based on the feedback loop. It aims to show that a representational paradigm is the product of a *misunderstanding of time* in the relation between epistemology and aesthetics, and that this misunderstanding stems from the projection of a cause-effect economy that reflects a specific

risis
epresentation
heterogeneity
rreversibility
new materialism
eedback loop

form of 'enframing', or paradigm, which inevitably enters a crisis when measured against change. That is, representation reflects an economy between sign and meaning (language-reality), a world organized around a cause-effect equation. From such a paradigm all interruptions or divergences from the zero-sum of the equation appear as a crisis.

First Question: The Crisis of Experience

When discussing representation, what are the differences and the implications occurring between the logic of reproducibility specific to *production* and the complex regime of *emergence* within networks? The problem is at least twofold: first it requires understanding technology not as a transparent vehicle, as neutral means to an end, but as a medium whose process of emergence generates language-specific and time sensitive dimensions, which install an 'aesthetic space'; that is, a specific set of possibilities and limitations. This, in turn, eludes both the linear subject-object equation of production and the closed necessity of the causality equation for an open *economy* where something else emerges, an *economy of the else* without necessity. The answer can be approached moving from Walter Benjamin's reading of *modernity* as a moment of crisis, in particular from his analysis of the concept of *technology*.[1]

Benjamin individuated a *divergence* between the existing order of things (culture) and the new technologies of modernity, which he tried to address via the necessity of the dialectical move. Yet, his analysis can be taken beyond dialectics. In Benjamin's reading, "technology is the mastery not of nature but of the relation between nature and man; (...) in technology, a *physis* is being organized through which mankind's contact with the cosmos takes a new and different form from that which it had in nations and families."[2] This understanding of technology as a form of *enframing*, which, differing from Heidegger's notion is intrinsically time sensitive,[3] shows technology as a *medium*:

---

1. The relation between technology and representation returns in several essays; here the main references are: Walter Benjamin, "The Work of Art in the Age of Mechanical Reproduction", in *Illuminations*, edited by Hannah Arendt, (London: Pimlico, 1999); Walter Benjamin, "To the Planetarium" and "The Author as a Producer", in *Selected Writings*, Vol. 1 and Vol. 2 of edited by M.W. Jennings, Harvard University Press, 1999; and "To The Planetarium", in *One Way Street*, Vol. 1, respectively edited by M.W. Jennings, (Cambridge, MA: Harvard University Press, 1999.)

2. Walter Benjamin, "To The Planetarium", 487.

3. See Martin Heidegger, "The Question Concerning Technology", in *The Question Concerning Technology and Other Essays*, edited by Joan Stambaugh and J. Glenn Gray, (London: Harper, 1977). For Heidegger, enframing (*Gestell*), is a form of "revealing", a mode of existence, a distribution of the world that comes to light already organized in economic terms, what he calls "standing reserve"; it almost acts as the scene on which modern technologies take place. However, enframing differs from Benjamin's analysis of technology insofar as it encompasses all technological phenomena and as such it is nothing technological.

not a neutral support representing meaning, but expressing specific sensual, political, and aesthetic properties. That is, engendering a language specific meaning, as Benjamin describes in his analysis of mechanical reproducibility. Technology thus becomes a *place* and a *discourse* at once, a set of dimensions, which requires and simultaneously generates a specific epistemology that is not absolute but, rather, is specific to the aesthetic space to which it refers.

This analysis lies within a wider question regarding the possibility of preserving the integrity of experience, which Benjamin sought to explain merging neo-Kantian concerns about the validity of the traditional table of categories with the materialist concept of the forces of production as the motor of history; which in turn led him to seek to "dialectically redeem the concept of experience, by finding an appropriate way of experiencing the crisis of experience itself;"[4] that is from inside experience escaping the a priori of the Kantian architecture. In this move the symmetry between transcendental forms of knowledge (epistemology) and experience (aesthetics), or subject and object, was already broken. Modernity as a moment of change is, for Benjamin, experienced as a crisis: a dichotomy between the old (existing social relations and traditional culture) and the 'new' (the potential implicit in technology). New forms of technology allow for, or have the *ability* to engender, values different to those expressed by traditional art / culture.

First Question Again

Following Benjamin's method, yet not his conclusions, one should ask how is it possible to address the crisis of experience from within experience; that is, retaining the phenomenological and materialist angles of the question while abandoning the necessity required by the dialectic move. Indeed, according to Benjamin the crisis stems from applying the wrong politico-epistemological structure to the present, in fact from the very application of an external theory onto history. Benjamin had defined the Kantian organization of the sensible in the transcendental aesthetic a 'mythology', based on the assumption or projection of a separation between subject and object.[5] Where does this leave the relationship between experience and reason? Is the present forced into representing the architecture of epistemology? There appears to be an incommensurable gap between the ephemeral forms of becoming and the

4. "Walter Benjamin", in The Stanford Encyclopedia of Philosophy (Spring 2011 Edition), Edward N. Zalta (ed.), URL = <http://plato.stanford.edu/archives/spr2011/entries/benjamin/>.

5. Walter Benjamin, "On the Program of the Coming Philosophy", in *One Way Street*, Vol. 1 of *Selected Writings*, edited by M.W. Jennings, (Cambridge, MA: Harvard University Press, 1999), 103.

transcendental forms of knowledge, which requires abandoning the opposition thesis-antithesis in favour of a different approach.[6]

Benjamin identifies a *paradigm shift* in the emergence of a new technology, which throws all expectations and projections about the world into a state of crisis; the crisis of an epistemology / ideology that can no longer support the a priori distinction between subject and object of knowledge, or sign and meaning as its paradigm. Thomas Kuhn's analysis of the behaviour of scientific paradigms helps to unravel the notion of crisis beyond the impasse reached by Benjamin's dialectical / messianic approach.[7] In Kuhn's argument science does not proceed by accumulation of knowledge, but through shifts of representational models of the world, where *anomalies* diverge from the paradigm until they appear as counter instances to the paradigm's very principle. While paradigms are projected as stable, anomalies revealed as *counter instances* are a moments of disorder and refloating where the established categories of a culture (its self-representation) appear no longer apt for the task of organizing the experience of the present. That is, the ontology of the wrong state of affairs leads to a crisis of expectations. But how did thought come to misrecognise the things it hoped to theorize?[8]

An *ontology* not of being but of *becoming*, throws a transcendental epistemology into a paradoxical state. In a paradigm shift ontology becomes unstable, yet it does not enter a process of sublation and synthesis with experience, rather it abandons the old paradigm (the past) for something *else*, without deterministic or economical equivalence. The absolute architecture of the forms of knowledge that Benjamin criticizes in Kant stems from the past becoming fossilized and assuming a position external to the present.[9] That is, pretending to explain change from an external point of observation not affected by it; a static position of *being* preserved from *becoming*, which projects and claims a hierarchy for its exclusive privilege, that of a metalanguage describing reality and ruling over it, thus perpetuating a metaphysical structure. The problem is to develop a logic that is not 'applied to' realty as a transparent theory (representation), and that does not engender a reading of reality already structured by its projected representation; but also

6. On this regard Laruelle proposes to distinguish a regime of 'modernity', one that always refers to a metaphysical code to which all reality must be related, from a 'contemporary' regime, which opens philosophy to reality requiring continuous redefinition. François Laruelle, "Towards a Philosophy We Can Deem Contemporary," Paper presented at the Swedenborg Society, (London, May 9, 2012).

7. Thomas Kuhn, *The Structure of Scientific Revolutions*, (Chicago: University of Chicago Press, 1962).

8. I am indebted to Dr. Mark Walker for this comment during several conversations.

9. Benjamin, "On the Program of the Coming Philosophy."

a logic that avoids the abyss of circular deferral produced by the returning 'always-already' introduced by postmodernity.

What is required is a move that does not foreclose the heterogeneity of the present and keeps practice and theory in a reciprocal relation of inter-causality. The question then is one of method: how can the integrity of experience be preserved, without rejecting the possibility of thought? Can the notion of *feedback loop* at play in complex systems be adopted as the logic of cohesiveness that generates meaning in the present, as synthetic but without necessity?

The 'suspension of the epistemological presupposition' of the neo-Kantian / phenomenological move opens the way for a regime of simultaneous converging and diverging serializations (technologies diverging from the existing epistemology and converging onto new discourses), which does not follow a teleology but synthesises retroactively, thus reversing the notion of temporality. While in representation there is a circular argument at play, which prevents understanding how meaning is established, serializations are heterogeneous regimes of emergence that escape the organization of the homogeneous code installed by a universal economy. That is, *a crisis is no longer an exception* to the equilibrium of the paradigm, rather it is intrinsic to the state of the present; the irreconcilable relation between converging and diverging series. These must not be mistaken for the traditional partition that keeps thought, epistemology, and the transcendental on one side and sensible and history on the other; a partition that implies that it is technology, or history, which diverges from epistemology and ontology. On the contrary, in a moment of change / crisis the emerging of new questions or distributions is not exclusively coming from the side of the sensible / experience; the 'new' can be a conceptual space as much as an sensual space. Indeed, it is not only technology, or experience, that 'runs ahead' and re-launches the questions of the paradigm in a new direction, as the materialist tradition proposes, rather it seems that it is the very logic of thought, when presenting itself as theory / epistemology (converging, defining, and closing), to be upset by escaping divergent series. Thus in a crisis the passage is from the anomaly of an epistemology in a paradoxical state, to an *ana-economy*, not in self-contradiction and in need of solution, but simply open.

But there is more. Beyond the first level of ontological instability, as Kuhn indicates, different paradigms install different sets of aesthetic-epistemological dimensions (aesthetic spaces), engendering specific questions for specific problems. They are incommensurable and irreconcilable. Proximity or simultaneity of paradigms does not guarantee a translation. There is no bridging between paradigms, only replacing. The lack of a space 'in between' is exactly where the crisis lays: the impossibility of an economy to engage with an open state, the morphing of an *open present*.

The question must be pushed past a linear oppositional logic between separate models of thought. A crisis is experienced because simultaneous divergent series are irreconcilable. Indeed, Kuhn points out that the passing from the stable state of a paradigm (normal science) to the next happens while the paradigm is in function, throwing science into an extraordinary state. The traditional 'in between' must be seen instead as a *moment of differentiation*; not A and B (or A=A for this matter), but *now* and *open*, the open present. The crisis is indeed the impossibility of smooth conversion; the lack of a third place between paradigms; the absence of an external or absolute code that permits the translation-transmission of information. There is no possibility of translating tradition into modernity, or analogue into network whilst preserving the previous capabilities and values, the equation is incomplete: it is just (x), the present, and openness. Normality (stable paradigms) borders the open. The extraordinary is a moment of divergence, not a third place on the background of two ordinary paradigms; it does not constitute a dualistic alterity with normal science. Rather it is the paradoxical state where the whole distribution of the sensible and epistemology must be reconfigured, the horizon where the present appears as a finite and yet unbound surface.

What then is the place of difference? It is necessary to ask what happens between the open and the dimensions of the universe of meaning. Is the open simply void? If the crisis must be addressed from inside experience, the event must have all of its causes and possibilities inside what happens, not elsewhere. If the open is just the returning of difference, difference must be part of the event; not outside, not something else, but the very lack of boundary to the happening of the event.

The technologies and discourses that reciprocally expand and articulate in the present are the dimensions of its identity; an instrument is nothing but a set of limitations (folds / dimensions), an absolutely smooth space would not allow any meaning to emerge. Rather than an economy between signifier and signified (or language and the world) sense emerges from the play amongst the possibilities of the very technologies in action, their *abilities*, and the conceptual space opened by discourses,[10] in an internal (*restricted*) economy whose values and meaning coincide with its grammar,[11] This is an *immersive*

10. Samuel Weber draws an interesting link between Benjamin and Derrida: *iteration*, the ability of a given technology to engender repetitions, becomes the motor that sets possible patterns in motion, allowing sense to take place. See Samuel Weber, *Benjamin's -abilities*, (Cambridge, MA: Harvard University Press, 2008), 3-19.

11. In *Philosophical Grammar*, Wittgenstein describes meaning as grammar: the play of a language not representing an external sense, but whose only denotation is the working of its internal rules. In other words the rules of language constitute the dimensions of its aesthetic space, effectively showing that a language is a technology and conversely that technology is a language. See Ludwig Wittgenstein, *Philosophical Grammar* (Berkley: University of California Press, 1974).

logic, which eludes the necessity of an external signification, and shows that technology is a discourse as much as discourses are sensual; the sensual as dimensions of meaning.

The First Real Question: The Now, Retroactivity and Time

Rather than concentrating on the dichotomy between aesthetics and epistemology (or technology and ideology) the focus should be the logic of emergence in the event: if the epistemological and aesthetic dimensions are generated in the event and if their logic is internal to it, that is, if epistemological and aesthetic dimensions coincide and expand in the extension of the event, then what happens to time?

Indeed, production and generation are divergent logics: the first follows a linear separation of subject-object in a process of accumulation, while the second is the result of a 'complex' move: the emergence generated by complex interactions whose properties were not implicit in the previous state of the system; a network logic, whose primary mode of operation is to open new links where there were none. This, rather than implementing pre-existing values, implies a retroactive form of synthesis based on a regime of reciprocity without the determinism of a linear cause-effect economy between discourses and practices, or between epistemology and aesthetic; a move not growing from an origin, but always from the 'now' (the present). The teleological linear time of Benjamin's expectations is here abandoned for the present as a moment of open transition.

If for Benjamin "*the present is defined as a time of crisis and transition*, and philosophical experience (truth) is associated with the glimpse within the present, via the past, of an utopian future that would bring history to an end",[12] this retaining the past into the future with a sublating synthesis postulates a teleological timeline where the present acts as a step in function to an end; 'standing in' on behalf of the future, representing it, effectively installing a economy between the past, the now, and what is yet to come. Whereas a process of emergence rather than containing these steps, *reassembles* the present into a new surface, in a process where statistical probability replaces necessity. Such emergence, a serialization or extension of patterns, is still mediation but retroactively, recognized as synthesis only from inside its specific dimensions once they are installed. Such new surface escapes both determinism and teleology and is incommensurable with the previous state. Here probability is not a time to come or a set of options to choose from,

12. Zalta, "Walter Benjamin", http://plato.stanford.edu/archives/spr2011/entries/benjamin/.

but openness. Emergence is the generation of a logic internal to the event, an event that takes place each time in different ways.

This implies an ecological move from teleology to a positive form of *enframing*. The redemption of experience that Benjamin sought cannot happen without a *simultaneous* reorganization of the forms of knowledge. That is, the logic of an event is the reciprocal organization of the distribution of the sensible and the articulation of epistemology in the extension of its dimensions. Here the enframing turns *positive*, it is an affirmative expansion of dimensions without 'outside'; the 'clearing', the coming into light of an horizon as the organization of the world, no longer constitutes a simultaneous concealing move, because all references to authenticity are abandoned if favour of emerging surfaces. Moreover, if for Heidegger a horizon conceals the authentic relationship to Being, which as authentic is also unique, an open present, which expands from the reciprocity and simultaneity of a complex logic, does not need to rest on a 'ground', on the contrary its being 'open' implies a plurality of possibilities of arrangements and distributions. The heterogeneity of probability supersedes linear necessity; other possibilities, other universes are not affected by the happening of the present one. The topical logicof cohesion of surfaces is an *ecology*, a constant re-distribution of an open equilibrium.[13]

The present as crisis, the 'now' is open. In an environment where time is not an arrow travelling from the past into the future (or 'present is not the future of a past', as Deleuze put it) and the synthesis of serialization is retroactive, the present is *always* a state of crisis. The emergence from complex interactions figures as crisis, since it changes the self-representation of the existing order of things without 'calling time'. It rearranges the present into a new paradigm, rather than answering previous questions. Thus the crisis is more than the impossibility of determinism, or unpredictability, it is heterogeneity seen from inside the paradigm of homogeneous representation.

Therefore a paradigm is an 'aesthetic space' (an articulation of the sensible and of epistemology), a *topos*; it has inner dimensions, which it has generated and it is constantly reaffirming. A paradigm acts as a *restricted economy*, whose values and exchanges are valid and limited only to its internal dimensions. Such economies are the internal or 'normal' side of the paradigm; they require a denial of the possibility of a critical state. Crisis instead is that which cannot be calculated, represented inside the existing system; it is the extraordinary

---

13. Regarding the notion of *ecology*, see Isabelle Stengers, *Cosmopolitiques 2*, (Paris: La Découverte, 1997).

moment opening onto the 'sovereign silence' of a general economy,[14] where incommensurability and heterogeneity are interrupting the equation.

In passing from a restricted economy (of cause-effect, thesis-antithesis, sign-meaning, built around a "=" sign resolvable in a "zero sum"),[15] to a general economy where something is lost for the lack of outer boundary, there is a *paradoxical economy*, which yields a different value (else) than the one expected; a crisis that indicates loss and gain, waste and value at the same time, yet not symmetric, but divergent, incommensurable and therefore irreconcilable. As such the crisis exposes the limits of representation. The equilibrium of a new ecology is an economy of the *else*, or *ana-economy*.

The crisis of experience is paradox rather than antithesis. Crisis is not an antithetic moment that lacks a synthetic solution, nor a matter of passing from state to state, but the moment of the same redistributing its dimensions. It is the paradox of a 'thesis / now' that changes without passing through an antithesis. Divergence reconceptualises the notion of crisis as de-territorializing while re-territorializing in a different direction. The paradox is not a return to a Humean scepticism, rather it stems from attempting to describe becoming from the point of view of being.

Paradoxes must be seen as moments of divergence and simultaneity. Indeed, the simultaneity of series in the paradox conceals a remixing, which is the operation of a *feedback loop*. In this returning the 'next round' will be different; that is, divergence taking place while still converging, yet converging differently each time, or converging as difference.[16] Kuhn had already seen this: "the decision to reject a paradigm is always the decision to accept another".[17] Out of the volatility of a delta of interpretations in a crisis only comes the restructuring of the question; a new 'fold', in the state of affairs, non-linear and non-necessary. Problems do not find synthetic solutions; rather they are superseded by new problems via a re-alignment of epistemological and aesthetic dimensions. A crisis is end and beginning at the same time, series diverging and converging on the same surface, in the same body-word. In the crisis the feedback loop generates new economies whose values are not measured against an absolute background but only internally. These are retroactive synthesis, not completions but the cohesion of a new ecological distribution / equilibrium, recognized as synthesis *a posteriori*, that is, only once they are installed.

---

14. See Jacques Derrida, "From Restricted to General Economy, an Hegelianism without reserve," in *Writing and Difference*, (London: Routledge, 1967).

15. The concept of "zero sum" has been introduced by Prof. Sue Golding during a cycle of seminars in 2010-2011.

16. See Gilles Deleuze, "Nietzsche," in *Pure Immanence; Essays on a Life*, 1965 (New York: Zone Books, 2001), 53-101.

17. Thomas S. Kuhn, *The Structure of Scientific Revolutions*, 77.

Therefore the anomaly is not the moment of crisis, but the economical representation of reality. In fact, the present is an open state or ana-economy where the incommensurable *else* emerges. This leads to another question:

Second Question: Dimensions, Dirty Passages and the Logic of *Elsewhere*

How passing from one paradigm's dimensions to another paradigm's dimensions takes place? If the open equation of a ana-economy installs incommensurable dimensions each time it returns, what happens when one paradigm is reconfigured into another? While 'sovereign silence' is the ultimate ana-economy, do local shifts retain some continuity or each shift drifts off into the infinity of the extraordinary?

The work of the feedback loop appears to be fuzzy. If experience cannot be 'reduced' to an absolute / transcendental code (that of a pure text, information code, or commodity); if there isn't an a-priori equation that permits a complete and even economic exchange, nor a clean and clear demarcation, then the passage will always be dirty, breaking edges, wasteful and mismatching, wasting potential, not matching every plug, USB, or shape; Wand at the same time it will require more and generate else than that which the previous system's dimensions could offer as potential or permit as limits. This breaking and meeting of different dimensions of meaning, is then as wasteful as it can be generative. Indeed, the crisis is not forever lost in a paradox; rather the emptiness of the sovereign silence of a general economy is the condition for the circulation of the feedback loop. The economical logic reconfigured as ecology shows a new distribution as *open distribution*, and the present as a state of disequilibrium. Yet, this does not make openness a resource as negativity is in Hegelian dialectic, nor it represents any form of dualism, rather it is the plain lack of the boundary of necessity. Ecology is the open equilibrium produced by *change within the same* and resting on disequilibrium; while productive and wasteful, it is always affirmative, *poietic*; it 'makes sense' (as Kuhn stated, there is no abandoning of one paradigm without already adopting another). Instead of a process of production based on cause-effect linearity, the ecology of a network is a matter of *emergence*; its logic is internal to the event, based on the event's dimensions and articulating them at the same time. Identity, the surface, is synthetized / mediated in the present as ecology: an *emergence of the present* in the *present* (this is not to say that historical crisis are necessarily painless, ecologies are not a happy Disneyland parks but *entangled* redistributions).

The present is open, in disequilibrium between time and chaosmos.[18] If epistemology is the representation / projection of a world of Being, inevitably it will run into a crisis when encountering unexpected data that refer to Becoming. Deleuze introduced the concept of chaosmos to indicate what is outside the organized linearity of this time-universe. Yet, chaosmos is only probability, not virtual or future to come, an open present; it implies a non-linear, non-teleological time being created in the passing from *chaos to order*.[19] The present is the heterogeneous moment where chaos and order coexist; a frontier between the organized / determined past (time) and chaos, which just for ease of description is called future. The open present is non representational and non economical (representation would be a present that must become future, or a future that must happen). Crisis is universality's inability to calculate multiversality, where the economy of past-future, energy-entropy, is always broken / open; in fact it was never whole. It does not yield what it was expected to produce in the past and at the same time it is generating something that the past had no necessity for, something that was not implicit in it. The feedback loop between order and chaos generates something new without necessity; in it, the present and time are generated together *retroactively*. Moreover, here the open is not the postmodern lack of ground, or infinite deferral, or the 'always-already' of a trace. It completely reverses the Cartesian deterministic mechanicism, without reintroducing void in the equation. Therefore, a crisis of experience requires a phenomenology directed not towards the 'thing itself', but towards the present: a *phenomenology of the surface*.

The paradigm shift is a heterogeneous 'portmanteau' moment for different series, a *domino turn* where one tile allows several simultaneous different directions, a crossroad of practices; it escapes or exceeds the existing paradigm, which produced the existing logic. In it incommensurability is the logical chaos between probability and time. In the heterogeneous paradox of divergence shifts are progressive nuances or messy crushes, not translations. Moreover there is no original state from which divergence moves, or a state of nature, or total noise; the event of sense is the crisis of another sense. One is always already immersed in language, one learns to speak and think while learning the dimensions of language / grammar.[20]

---

18. Gilles Deleuze, "Series 24," *The Logic of Sense*, trans Charles Stivale (London: Continuum, 1990).

19. Ilya Prigogine & Isabelle Stengers, *From Chaos to Order*, (London: HarperCollins, 1985). On this regard John Gribbin's notion of multiverse is also interesting, in particular the description of time / entropy in the second law of thermodynamics: without irreversible changes in the system there is no 'passing' of time. See also: John Gribbing, *In Search of the Multiverse*, (Penguin: London, 2009).

20. See Lyotard's critique of St. Augustine's semiotic theory, in François Lyotard, *Libidinal Economy*, trans Iain Hamilton Grant, (London, Continuum, 2004), Chapter 2, 43-94.

The new surface generated by the simultaneous converging while diverging is in excess of an economy; converging-diverging act as vectors 'pulling' in different directions from one point, which is not a centre at rest but is created by these tensions between disequilibrium and probability. These simultaneous movements generate time / space rather than being located in them. Interestingly Althusser had already approached the event of revolution as a critical threshold where the simultaneous alignment of several different segments or variables at their critical level of intensity generates change;[21] yet, in spite of the similarity, topological emergence takes place without the support of an external timeline; in fact the synthesis a posteriori of complexity logic installs an aesthetic temporality which is a *poietic* form of time. Multiple vectors and disequilibrium create time and space.

Indeed, heterogeneity escapes economies not on the background of time, but in making time. The passage between economy and economy exposes the open general economy or openness that (ana)envelops them. The present / meaning is tangent to chaos, an extraordinary moment of quantum openness, which clashes with the paradigm of determinism and representation. It is not a matter of a leap into 'nothing', rather just reaching the 'end' of one paradigm's set of dimensions. That is, the logic of becoming is internal to the event; it opens with it, yet with out the authenticity that Heidegger sought, rather each time differently. Such extraordinary leap threatens the authority of the language-paradigm for a multitude of meaningful practices, which, rather than seeking a 'ground', are finding local passages, internal links, and temporary bridges to generate value and escape. In this light, since it abandons both the ideology of the possibility of an ultimate object of knowledge and the notion of a *noumenon*, the articulation of epistemology not only coincides with the distribution of the sensible, but ~ as Rancière describes ~ shows that the aesthetic dimensions of the phenomenon are intrinsically political.[22]

In writing the laws there is always a risk of foreclosing the present. If the heterogeneity of the event is not preserved, an installed theory in its process of normalization will pronounce laws representing the paradigm as a priori. A crisis will be regarded as an exception and normalization will re-close the open gap, re-mark the boundary of the paradigm-society, re-construct a whole; performing, that is, a process of inclusion-exclusion where the possibility of difference is entirely silenced, made not to exist. Questions that *cannot be asked*, that are outside the paradigm's equation, become non-problems, invisible. However it is important to stress that this cannot be deemed the

---

21. Luis Althusser and Étienne Balibar, *Reading Capital*, trans Ben Brewster, 1970, http://www.marxists.org/reference/archive/althusser/1968/reading-capital/index.htm. Accessed 14 October 2012.

22.See Jacques Rancière, *The Politics of Aesthetics*, (London: Continuum, 2000).

alienation of an originary state,[23] rather it is the separation of thought from the sensible, or the separation of meaning from the language that produces it; a separation that will always create a political divide and limit access to the existing discourse to those who are already included, as Rancière shows in his discussion of the politics of aesthetics.[24]

Conclusions: A New Form of Materialism

The question then focuses on the *inside* of the event, *emergence* is a logic in itself, which abandons the spatialization of time for the temporalization of an aesthetic space as incommensurable: a place that is without representing, a *topos*. Indeed, if the event is change / becoming, rather than teleological development, then it does not need an 'outside'. A ana-economy is an *affirmative* event, it is the moment that differentiate *sense* from *silence*, not from non-sense. The causes and elements of change are all internal to the event, and they can take place because of openness. This is at the same time more complex and simpler than the 'returning of difference'. The specific / inner logic of incommensurable economies means that each event's internal logic emerges from the interactions of the elements that constitute it; that is, the elements that constitute the present. Deleuze resorted to the '*univocity* of events', a transcendental space of pure difference, to explain becoming.[25] Yet, the fact that the event can happen rests only on it *not being bound*, open; the 'cause', how the event happens is site-specific, internal, and therefore retroactive. As such the *eventum tantum* excludes any totalizing argument, it is finite but not bound, a ana-totality.

In the case of the shift from analogue to digital operations, from production to generation, the passage must really be seen behaving in the light of the rhizome: a heterogeneity whose dimensions take place by subtraction: 'n-1';[26] where 'n' is the infinity of probability. As such the synthetic meaning /

23. This is a problem that to some extent seems to taint Luce Irigaray's argument in her critique of Heidegger, where logos' rigour silences a fluid movement. See Luce Irigaray, *The Forgetting of Air in Martin Heidegger*, trans Mary Beth Mader (Austin: University of Texas Press, 1999). A similar problem is at the base of Agamben's analysis which finds 'the exceptional' always being present at both 'ends' of the law (i.e., at the origin and moment of application). See respectively Giorgio Agamben, *Stato di Eccezione ~ Homo Sacer 2*, (Torino: Bollati Boringhieri, 2003), and *Che cos'è un Dispositivo*, (Roma: Nottetempo, 2006).

24. In this regard, Foucault's continuity of regimes of power through the ~ alleged ~ exceptional state of war and the stable periods of peace is correct. Indeed, it is representation that makes the state appear, by marking a boundary, and installing an equation or code to guarantee the organization of an otherwise heterogeneous surface. See Michel Foucault, *Society Must be Defended*, trans David Macey (London: Penguin, 2004), Seminar 2 and Seminar 3.

25. Gilles Deleuze, *Logic of Sense*, Series 24, trans Charles Stivale (London, Continuum, 1990).

26. Gilles Deleuze & Félix Guattari, "1. Rhizome: Introduction," in *A Thousands Plateaux*, trans

present is always mediated, but not teleological. The poietic logic of emergence introduces a new philosophy of history based on the affirmative logic of the medium / technology. This abandons both scientific determinism and the 'determinism' of a strict materialistic analysis for a regime of *emergence of the present in the present*. A point in space, a moment in history, or a concept in thought are no longer anchored to a main meta-narrative nor lost in the abyss, rather self-generating it via resonances and interferences.

Postscript on Value: Definition of Value: Process Only ~ Network Economy

The passage from chaos to order as described by Prigogine-Stengers returns in Kuhn analysis of paradigm's behaviour as something that has value not because it is absolute, or is measured against an absolute, but because it functions, it is *cohesive*; because, albeit for a while only, it creates links with other parts, which allow flow, exchange, circulation, correspondences and ~ most importantly ~ the creation of new links within the network. Process is all there is to the notion of value and meaning. Value is what is implementable in a discourse according to its dimensions and reciprocally as one of its dimensions.

Ultimately, Deleuze's shift from traditional western logic, which based its hierarchy on nouns-subjects, to verbs (gerunds and infinitives) and their declinations converging on body / subjects is a logic of series and patterns that *generates space / time* rather than happening on their background. Hence *individuation* is the convergence, the temporary resonance of segments with the same frequency, the temporary alignment of different patterns. Economies, representations, translation are not between simultaneous values, but between the present and the past in the inner logic of each event: "*one is always smaller than what one is becoming, and bigger than what one was*".[27] Therefore, in the *eventum tantum*, the passing from chaos to order requires, or only permits, a *phenomenology* of the present. The 'thing itself' is the surface, the present, not a logical depth, while the past is the epistemological presupposition that tends to foreclose it. In the logic of heterogeneous emergence the artistic coincides with the political; indeed it should be noted that after the *Logic of Sense* Deleuze arrives at the *Logic of Sensation* not as a different kind of logic, but as the only logic possible: that of some specific works of a specific artist, rather than of art as a whole.

Mattia Paganelli

Brian Massumi, (London: Continuum, 2004), 3-25.

27. Deleuze, "Series 1," *Logic of Sense*, [My italics].

The 9th Technology of Otherness:

A Certain kind of Debt[1]

Abstract: Classical metaphysics requires a concept of the ethical that belies or erases certain forms of truth-telling, often pulling the ethical in the direction of more sterilized forms of reason and rationality in order to invoke its universal applicability as a kind of 'one-size-fits-all' for any person, place, time, or thing. In so doing, not only does this tend to diminish or expunge the sensuous, carnal encounters of body and spirit, it pre-figures certain forms of courage, care and imagination so that the very core of what it means to make a community alive, responsive, and creative remains stuck in the old classical canons of thought and practice. In this way, the beliefs and 'truths' that tend to be reproduced serve only to strengthen the status quo's status ~ somewhat of a problem if that status quo's status is also mired in misogynist, homophobic, ethnic and / or racially divisive traditions. The 9th Technology of Otherness, *building upon Foucault's Courage of Truth, the last lecture series before his untimely death, seeks to show how an ethics drawn along the sensuous modalities (as Foucault positions them) of courage (parrhēsia) and curiosity (zētēsis), creates a certain form of community, a certain kind of self, and with it, a certain kind of debt. It is precisely this debt that Socrates reminds Crito 'not to forget to remember to pay' to Asclepius, and to do so with the now quite infamous gift of the bird-cock.*

> And the man who gave Socrates the poison now and then looked at his feet and legs and after a while he pressed his foot hard, and asked "him if he could feel; and he said, No; and then his leg, and so upwards and upwards, and showed us that he was cold and stiff. And Socrates felt them himself, and said: When the poison reaches the heart that will be the end. He was beginning to grow cold about the groin, when he uncovered his face, for he had covered himself up, and said ~ they were his last words ~ he said: Crito, I owe a cock [έναν κόκορα] to Asclepius; will you remember to pay the debt? ~ Plato, Phaedo.[2]

1. "The 9th Technology of Otherness" was commissioned by Henry Rogers for his edited collection, *Queer Textualities*, (London / Birmingham: ARTicle Press / OSB Publishing, 2013). It is gratefully reprinted here with the Editor's permission.

2. Plato, *Phaedo: The Last Hours of Socrates*, trans Benjamin Jowett, (The Project Gutenberg Ebook: 2008). Updated Jan 15, 2013 at http://www.gutenberg.org/files/1658/1658-h/1658-h.htm. Translations vary as to whether Socrates is purported to have used "I" or "we" with respect to the owing of the cock to Asclepius. We will keep the Gutenberg translation but later in the argument will draw upon Foucault's use of 'we' to develop a more general point about the care of the self especially in relation to the true.

thics
conomy of debt
ourage; *parrhēsia*
uriosity; *zētēsis*
ueer difference
agic garden
ird-cock

Strange Debt

The question of debt, especially as the last words Socrates was purported to have whispered moments before he succumbed to the hemlock, remains a vexed and oddly intractable one; perhaps even more so when encountered initially amongst writings in a book on queer sensibilities. But it may not be as strange as it might at first appear and, indeed, as we shall see after dispatching with two of the more well-known interpretations, it may at least begin to provide an initial glimpse into a heterogeneic 'post-' postmodern ethics, one fuelled by a particular kind of debt, generated by a certain curiosity (zētēsis), and propelled by a queer, strange, sexual-carnal / ethical-political-aesthetic truth (parrhēsia).[3] It is a blood-debt poetics, this oddly lubricated economy, with ethical difference at its core, courage as its trope and a communal 'care of the self' as its technology ~ what we will name as the 9th technology of otherness.

Before developing that intricate claim, let us turn briefly to Nietzsche and then to Derrida. In one of the most famous interpretations of Socrates' dying words, Nietzsche concludes, along with many others, that because Asclepi us was the God of Healing and because the very last words on the mind of Socrates was to ask Crito not to forget to pay off, as Nietzsche would phrase it, a "ridiculous debt" to this (and no other) god, Socrates seemed to have undergone a deathbed conversion ~ one born out of a fear of dying, belying, thought Nietzsche, a grave and deeply secretive pessimism. For Nietzsche, this was the complete reversal of all Socrates stood for during the whole of his life.

> This ridiculous and terrible 'last word' means for those who have ears: "O Crito, life is a disease." Is it possible that a man like him, who had lived cheerfully and like a soldier in the sight of everyone, should have been a pessimist? He had merely kept a cheerful mien whilst concealing all his life long his ultimate judgment, his inmost feeling. Socrates, Socrates suffered life! And then he still revenged himself ~ with this veiled, gruesome, pious, and blasphemous saying. Did a Socrates need such revenge? Did his overrich virtue lack an ounce of magnanimity? ~ Alas, my friends, we must overcome even the Greeks![4]

3. A point to which we will return momentarily, but see: Michel Foucault, "15 February, The First Hour," in his *The Courage of Truth: The Government of Self and Others II, Lectures at the Collège de France 1983-1984*, trans Graham Burchell, (New York: Palgrave-Macmillan, 2011), 86-89. Note: the Socratic form of *parrhēsia* (ethos) carefully sidesteps the carnal-knowledge practice of body, sex, sweat ~ but as we will see, this is not just an 'interesting' aspect of queer *parrhēsia*, it is its verification.

4. Friedrich Nietzsche, "The Dying Socrates," in his *The Gay Science (with a Prelude in Rhymes and an Appendix of Songs)*, translated with commentary by W. Kaufman, (New York: Vintage, 1974), section 340, 272. The earlier part of the aphorism gives the full sense of his disappointment: "I admire the courage and wisdom of Socrates in everything he did, said ~ and did not say. This mocking and

On a rather different note, Derrida's interpretation(s) announce a multiple doubling of an inheritance / debt, an inscription of a last will and testament by a dying man (Socrates) whose words are recorded by someone (Plato) who, despite not even being present at the moment of utterance ~ apparently he was sick on the day ~ must nevertheless suppose a memory (or, in any case, a 'not forgetting') of an event which may or may not have taken place, by someone whose authority he wishes to break but, by writing those last words, instead immortalizes that very authority. Plato, caught as both receiver & sender, is now also con-joined to Socrates "from behind" by virtue of the reciprocating journeying inheritance of inscription.[5] Here the end-game becomes a double entendre mid-game and in so doing, entirely changes the rules of the game. As Derrida so vividly (and oddly homo-cidally) enframes it: Socrates could be said to be eternally fucked by a Plato who may or may not be aware of what he is doing and indeed must do. Plato: the devoted pupil-inheritor on the one hand, the knowledge-transfer disseminator on the other; receiver and sender, Plato enacts the double-bind which looks a lot like an innocent placebo but generates the pleasure / pain sadomasochism of the pharmakon. And all the while, the debt-cock just keeps on growing.

Over to Derrida:

> 5 June 1977. [...] I have not yet recovered from this revelatory catastrophe. Plato behind Socrates. Behind he has always been, as it is thought, but not like that. Me, I always knew it, and they did too, those two I mean. What a couple. Socrates turns his back to Plato

---

enamored monster and pied piper of Athens, who made the most overweening youths tremble and sob, was not only the wisest chatterer of all time: he was equally great in silence. I wish he had remained taciturn also at the last moment of his life; in that case he might belong to a still higher order of spirits. Whether it was death or the poison or piety or malice ~ something loosened his tongue at that moment and he said; "O Crito, I owe Asclepius a rooster." This ridiculous and terrible 'last word' means for those who have ears: "O Crito, *life is a disease*."

5. See for example 4 September 1977 where Derrida explains: "When Being is thought *on the basis of* the gift of the *es gibt* (sorry for the simplifying stenography, this is only a letter), the gift itself is not something; it would be, hmmm, like an *"envoi"*, destination, the destinality, sorry, of an *envoi*, which of course does not send this or that, which sends nothing that is, nothing that is a "being," a "present." [...] in Jacques Derrida, *The Postcard: From Socrates to Freud and Beyond,* trans by Alan Bass, (Chicago / London: University of Chicago Press, 1987), 61. But for the multiplicity / doubling of inscription andits circulation see also *Of Grammatology,* trans G. Spivak, (Baltimore: The Johns Hopkins University Press, 1974 / 1997), especially Part I "Writing Before the Letter," 3-94; *The Gift of Death,* trans David Wills (London / Chicago: University of Chicago Press, 1996), especially Chapters 2 and 3 ("Beyond: Giving for the Taking, Teaching and Learning to Give, Death," and "Whom to Give to (Knowing Not to Know), 35-52 and 53-81, respectively. Also see *The Politics of Friendship,* trans George Collins, (London: Verso, 2005), especially Chapter 4, "The Phantom Friend Returning (in the name of Democracy), 75-112. Last but not least, his seminal *Dissemination* (New York: Continuum, 1981), especially regarding the pharmakon developed in "Plato's Pharmacy," 67-122; and "The Double Session," 187ff.

> who has made him write what he wanted while pretending to receive it from him. [...] And since Plato writes, without writing, without wanting that a trace be preserved, since he writes, without writing, that Socrates, who passes for someone who has never written, in truth will have written, whether this is known (or not) and will have written just that which he will have written (but who, he?), you can try to forward the inheritance...
>
> 5 September 1977. [...] P.S. I have again overloaded them with colors, look, I made up our couple, do you like it? Doubtless you will not be able to decipher the tattoo on plato's prosthesis, the wooden third leg, the phantom-member that he is warming up under Socrates' ass.[6]

Of course there are other interpretations to the last words of Socrates, though most of which, over the past two millennium+ of discussion thus far, tend to fall under the two broad headings as singled out above. That is, of a less than benign, suspicious or secretive 'final thought confession' or 'deathbed conversion'; or, as expressing however enigmatically, a pharmakon-esque inscription of Being, woven into the very fabric of time, circulation, inheritance and debt, and therewith crucial to the (quasi-) transcendental movement of a trace, any trace ~ be it identity, sexuality, democracy, or indeed, life itself.

Changing the Value of Currency (a certain kind of courage)

Foucault proposes a wholly distinct approach from the broad outlines sketched above. It is one that, as we will see, not only introduces a methodological game-changer, but opens onto a completely different environ, quite distinct from the one encountered by Adam & Eve and their deeply troubled progeny.

In the immediate months preceding his death in 1984, Foucault delivered a series of 18 lectures at the Collège de France, published posthumously (in French, 2008 and in English, 2011) as The Courage of Truth: The Government of Self and Others, II.[7] These lectures were a continuation of the previous two years lectures (from 1982 and 1983) and were situated around four practice-knowledge hubs or modalities of truth: (1) the modality of prophecy/religiosity; (2) the modality of the order of things; that is, of being (phusis); (3) the modality of demonstrative technique or tekhne in the narrow sense of 'expertise' and finally, (4) the modality that polemicized the

6. *The Postcard*, 12 and 65, respectively. Italicization in the original.
7. Foucault, *The Courage of Truth*, 89.

human condition (ethos).[8] It was to this last economy of truth, itself a particular knowledge-practice form of parrhēsia, that Foucault begins to tease out what is at stake in the elliptical demand of Socrates to Crito: that Crito 'must remember not to forget' to repay the debt owed to Asclepius in the manner of gifting the cock.[9] As we shall see shortly, it is from the 'certain kind of debt' this fourth modality exposes, reiterates and promotes that the 9th technology of otherness is created and sustained.

Invoking the motto of Diogenes to re-situate the entire polemic of debt and the multitude interpretations of its meaning via Socrates, Crito, Asclepius and the cock, Foucault steps away from the iterative fact of exchange, circulation and debt ~ let's just call it 'the market community' ~ and, instead demands, as did Diogenes, that if you (read: we) cannot alter the fact of exchange itself, then at least, to quote Diogenes, "change the value of the currency" [Αλλάξει την αξία του νομίσματος].[10] The currency in question could be said to be the general economy of truth; its value: the polemical condition of being human (ethos). Its parrhēsia, Foucault argues, is a truth forged from the complex and yet completely obvious mix of curiosity, sensate, invention, experimentation, practice, bodily knowledge, power, movement and risk. It is this truth that could (and did) change the currency; it is this truth that could (and did) emit a different kind of ethics; it is this truth that could (and did) draw a certain kind of debt; it is this truth that could (and did) shift the terrain of aesthetics from 'the Beautiful and Sublime' to that of an unquantifiable strange / estranged ethos. And it is this truth that required ~ and still requires ~ courage, because it is this truth that could rock (and did rock and still does rock) the status quo.

> "We can say then, very schematically, that the parrhēsiast is not the prophet who speaks the truth when she reveals fate enigmatically in the name of someone else. The parrhēsiast is not a sage who, when she wants to and, against the background of her silence, tells of being and nature (phusis) in the name of wisdom. The parrheisast is not the professor or teacher, the expert who speaks of tekhne in the name of a tradition. So she does not speak of fate, being or tekhne. Rather,

---

8. See the whole of "1 February 1984: First Hour" and "1 February 1984: Second Hour," *The Courage of Truth*, but particularly 15-19 and 25-27, respectively.

9. The general outlines of the concept *parrhēsia* are developed throughout the series of lectures on *The Courage of Truth*, but for this point see in particular, "Lecture One: 1 February 1984: First Hour," 1-22, and especially 10ff, as well as the afterword "The Course Context," *The Courage of Truth*, 343-358.

10. "7 March 1984, The Second Hour," in *The Courage of Truth*, 226-228.

> inasmuch as she takes the risk of provoking war with others [...] the parrhēsiast brings into play the true discourse of what the Greeks called ethos."[11]

For parrhēsia to exist in the sense Foucault is developing means first that there must be some kind of bond between the statement's sender and the receiver. Second, there must be some kind of risk to the exposing of truth on the part of the speaking subject, ranging from the breaking up of a relationship to the violent retaliation of the State. Hence, the parrhēsiast and the ethos 'to tell it as it is' requires a certain kind of courage and risk. It is the courage to speak out, to provoke, to incite into action without taking oneself out of the relationship; to invent anew by supposing 'it could be otherwise' and then figuring out what and how this 'otherwise' might become real, alive, take root and flouish, without preventing the 'telling it as it is' from being heard even if it might wound or destroy the 'messenger'. Not shock for shock's sake; not offence just because it could be done; not a sterile rationality backing any decision; but rather, a certain kind of connection, a certain kind of care and attention to detail; a certain kind of courage, curiosity, stylistics of existence, generosity, intellect, humour ~ call it what you will ~ a complex/heterogeneic logic of sense to make 'it' known; to make 'it' happen, to make manifest a 'certain kind of practice-knowledge' of that which may not 'fit in' exactly or precisely (or even at all), but in spite of that (or even because of it), may put one's body and soul at risk to make that polemical condition of life itself accessible, hearable, readable, graspable, right here, right now.[12]

---

11. "1 February 1984, The Second Hour," *The Courage of Truth*, 25. The word 'she' has been used instead of the traditional translation of 'he' when the genitalia really should not matter to the argument; and, not to put too fine a point on it, in order to provoke 'a war with others.' (JG).

12. See "1 February 1984: The First Hour," in *The Courage of Truth*, 11, where Foucault details it this way: "The parrhēsiast gives his opinion, he says what he thinks, he personally signs, as it were, the truth he states, he binds himself to this truth, and he is consequently bound to it and by it. But this is not enough. For after all, a teacher, a grammarian or a geometer, may say something true about the grammar or geometry they teach, a truth which they believe, which they think. And yet we will not call this *parrhēsia*. We will not say that the geometer and grammarian are parrhēsiasts when they teach truths which they believe. For there to be *parrhēsia*, you recall ~ I stressed this last year ~ the subject must be taking some kind of risk [in speaking] this truth which he signs as his opinion, his thought, his belief, a risk which concerns his relation with the person to whom he is speaking. For there to be *parrhēsia* in speaking the truth one must open up, establish and confront the risk of offending the other person, of irritating him, of making him angry and provoking him to conduct which may even be extremely violent. [...] In short, the act of truth, requires: first, the manifestation of a fundamental bond between the truth spoken and the thought of the person who spoke it; second, a challenge to the bond between to interlocutors... Hence this new feature of *parrhēsia*: it involves some form of courage."

The Queering of Difference

Now this parrhēsia, this ethical commitment 'to tell it as it is' was not, and could not, be made in isolation. In the example cited above, clearly the courage to speak was immersed in / born of a profound commitment, connectedness, a friendship of the self to (another / an-other) self. It required a courage buoyed or infused with the political, aesthetic, possibly dirty and unimaginable right 'to know' (thyself) in relation to this self-other. In so knowing, telling, making, doing, a radical, slightly more subtle heterogeneic form of the ethical was now being advanced by Foucault, one where the veridiction of the parrhēsiastic ethos, would be (and must be) maintained as an 'always-already' plurality of self-to-self collective connectedness.

This heterogeneic plurality of 'self' exposed yet another set of multiplicities. For parrhēsia of the fourth modality encounter, requires in the founding / finding of this ethical multiplicity ~ this economy of living ~ a recognition on both 'sides' of the self-to-self relation that a particular governance or care must take place. This governance not only concerned the quality of life itself: that in order for the (heterogeneic / pluralised) self to survive and, indeed, thrive, a radical governance or care of the self, brought to bear by 'telling it as it is', must always remain critically embedded into one's relational being in the world. But it also meant that this embeddeness, this ethical 'currency' must somehow be repeated; must somehow be 'circulated' time after time. And as it was premised on, indeed required a public 'other' ~ neither priest, nor teacher nor technician, nor police ~ but rather the parrahēsiac 'other', to tend to and to nourish, this generative and pluralised 'self-to-self' care, it was this recognition and insistence of this kind of care of self, that forms the context to Socrates' elliptical remark 'not to forget' what most people tended to forget or did not even know it should be remembered: the pluralised ethical demand to care for the pluralised self. "No longer political bravery," writes Foucault, "but ... the introducing [of] a certain form of truth into a knowledge that men do not know they know, a form of truth which will lead them to take care of themselves." Thus, he continues:

> "I tried to show you how, in his Apology, Socrates defined his parrhēsia, his courageous truth-telling, as a truth-telling whose final objective and constant concern was to teach men to take care of themselves. Socrates took care of men, but not in the political form: he wants to take care of them so that they will learn to take care of themselves."[13]

13. "15 February 1984: The Second Hour," in *The Courage of Truth*, 110.

Returning, then to the curious debt owed to Asclepius, to be paid in terms of the bird-cock. As is well known, a debt of this nature is charged when and only when a specific body is known to be gravely ill, then healed (by Asclepius) and the resultant 'thank you' is manifested precisely as cited above. But in the last moments of Socrates' life, there is no (apparent) diseased body; and thus there is no (apparent) healing; so why the payback, why the insistence to 'remember not to forget' and why link it to courage, the 'courage to tell the truth (parrhēsia)? It is because Socrates, as a living parrhēsiast becomes in death, both parrhēsiast and payback, the embodied ana-materiality of a polemicized ethics.

To put this slightly differently, it is because, this 'certain kind of truth' is nothing more nor less than the Socratic prick that both lances the boil of a forgetting / concealing (with minor apologies to Heidegger), whilst simultaneously goading into action a pluralized 'care of the self', and with it, a profoundly heterogeneic economy of being, what could be called a 'magic garden' which must be tended to, cultivated, over and again. For magic gardens do not happen on their own; they require a profound willingness (courage) to engage in the dangerous game of 'telling it as it is', and remembering not to forget to pay the debt in the currency of a multi-dimensional, multi-relational 9th technology of otherness.

Johnny Golding

Discourse in a Coma:

A Comment on a Comma in the Title of Lyotard's *Discourse, Figure*

Abstract: One of the key claims in Jean-François Lyotard's Discourse, Figure *is that the dialectical method (the backbone of Western philosophy) tends to obscure and hide all which is invisible, illegible and sensual. Lyotard's strategy in exposing this rift within language (and philosophy) is by way of showing that the distance between the sign and the referent should not be thought of as negation but as a form of expression. Instead of the dialectical relation between the image and the object Lyotard proposes radical heterogeneity that he names 'thickness'. This paper examines Lyotard's non-dialectical approach in relation to the title of the book and argues that the comma is positioned as the sensual technology that creates the possibility of discursive continuity.*

One of the recurrent themes of the Western philosophical canon is the distinction between sensual perceptions and rational knowledge. Since Plato established the dialogue as the form of his philosophical method, discourse ~ in the twofold sense of an utterance and the toing and froing of an argument ~ is the name of the technology that is able to extract true knowledge from experience. As the discussion in the Republic helps to explain, perceptions are inherently unreliable and deceptive because the senses are prone to errors and illusions. Only the rational discourse has the tools to overcome illusions and to point towards true knowledge. For instance, perception suggests that a figure in the distance is smaller than it really is. Yet, the application of logical reasoning will reveal that the figure only appears small because it obeys the laws of geometrical perspective. Nevertheless, even after the perspectival correction is applied, the figure still appears small and the truth of the matter is revealed not in the perception of the figure but in its rational representation in a discourse.

It is precisely because discourse is the guarantor of truth that it marks both the very possibility of knowledge and the limit beyond which knowledge cannot go. Whatever cannot be rationally represented in a discourse remains outside of knowledge and immune to it. To know the truth about something means to be able to represent it, and the proclivity for representation is an indication of a sound and rational mind. For this reason discourse carries within it the stamp of self-validating certainty: the subject of a discourse is rational because rationality is the technique of the discourse. On the other hand, precisely because the subject has to be validated through representation, whatever belongs to perception remains unknown to the subject.[1] Therefore,

oma
omma
yotard
hickness
ensual technology
adical heterogeneity
anguage rifts
ign and referent

1. Claire Colebrook speaks about the paradox of representation with exemplary clarity: "[...] the threshold of representation not only marks modernity off from its darker past (when law was imposed

,

discourse can be understood as the distillation of ideas from experience. Experience however is not made of ideas but of a mixture of ideas and perceptions and while ideas can be represented, perceptions can be only sensed.[2]

In *Discourse, Figure* Lyotard is concerned to correct the one-sidedness of the western philosophical canon by suggesting that despite appearances, irrational forces are raging under the veneer of reason and discourse is unable to fully rid itself from dependence on fallible and unreliable perceptions. Taking up linguistics as the case in point, Lyotard seems to be saying that what is wrong with linguistics is not its tools or methods but that it considers language in terms of discourse:

Linguistics marks the moment when language takes itself as object. So long as it positions itself at the tip of the aim [visée], it obscures itself as designated: linguistic discourse is thus a discourse that draws the night over discourse.[3]

Understood correctly, language is precisely the product of the irresolvable tension between discourse and figure, or between representation and perception. A study of language worthy of its name must take account of this difference as the productive and creative force that holds discourse and figure in suspended animation. For this reason the "," (comma) in the title of the book is ~ figurally speaking ~ the key to the book. Is the comma (",") part of the discourse or is it a figure? Can the comma be considered purely as a representation, or is it something other than a symbol? The comma appears to belong to both registers at once: it is a linguistic sign that operates according to the conventions of syntax and it is also something else entirely, it is a slowing down, a brief pause that introduces a rupture within the discursive continuity. The comma in *Discourse, Figure* exposes the inescapable paradox that indicates the limits of the discourse by suggesting that rationality can only be maintained through its dependence on the outside of rationality. The comma is a punctuation sign, it indicates a hiatus. The purpose of the discourse is to harness perceptions and to organise them in a way that allows for systemic and structured representation of knowledge. However, the comma

---

from without); the threshold of representation scars modernity itself, occurring as a limit within the possibility of modernity. [...] modern philosophy situates itself within the representational limits of the subject. Representation is a condition of finitude. Because knowledge is received from without it must be taken up and re-presented. What can be known is therefore determined and delimited by the representational powers of the subject." Claire Colebrook, *Ethics and Representation: From Kant to Post-structuralism.* (Edinburgh: Edinburgh University Press, 1999), 1.

2. On this point see Deleuze's lectures on Spinoza "Lectures by Gilles Deleuze On Spinoza." http://deleuzelectures.blogspot.co.uk/2007/02/on-spinoza.html (accessed July 16, 2012).

3. Jean-François Lyotard, *Discourse, Figure* trans Antony Hudek and Mary Lydon (Minneapolis: University of Minnesota Press, 2011), 100.

introduces a pause, the pause opens a gap and the gap allows for perception to sneak back into the discourse. What is being established by the comma is an opening that offers the possibility of play: it creates an interruption that makes it possible to have a choice. The choice is to continue with one series or with another. Chronologically the comma comes before the Figure, but it recovers a figure right inside the discourse. This sensual contraband is not imported into the discourse from outside but is found at the same place where the sign, representation and logos reside. For Lyotard this is a key strategy in dismantling the sovereignty of the logos:

Are we talking about another sort of sign? Not in the slightest, they are the same as those with which the semiotician carries out his theory and textual practice. The first thing to avoid, comrades, is to claim that we have taken up a position somewhere else. We're not moving out of anywhere, we're staying right here, we occupy the terrain of signs [...].[4]

Discourse, Figure is a discourse about discourse, but it is not a meta-discourse. There is no such thing as a representation of representation. Lyotard is not suggesting a meta-language with which to speak about "Discourse" because this would be tantamount to falling back into representation. Instead, he locates the sensible, the affective and the figurative in the pause indicated by this mark ",". The comma is not the ground of the discourse, neither it is an Archimedean point located outside of it, rather it is the differential between logos and perception. Understood from the perspective of the comma, Discourse is not an articulation of externally given reality but a relation between two forces. It is the continuous variation in this relation, the modulation between logos and affect that accounts for the creation of sense. The comma situates multiplicity, affect and duration right inside the discourse. Association with the comma exposes discourse itself as infinitesimally variable and therefore undecidable. In the same time it also means that there is at least a part of the discourse that might resist being absorbed into representation. Questions such as "is this a true or false statement?" do not apply to the comma as it is neither true or false. Comma is almost ethical rather than aesthetic: it refuses to signify and yet it strives to be of use, to be put to work.

What does it take to rethink the discourse from the perspective of the comma? In coming to address the paradoxical condition of the discourse Lyotard claims that what is required is nothing less than a revolution in language and philosophy. Rather then arguing for the domination of logos over sense or of sense over logos, Lyotard suggests that in order to prevent the triumph of idealism discourse has to be reconfigured as the difference between

---

4. Jean-Francois Lyotard, *Libidinal Economy* trans Iain Hamilton Grant (London: Continuum, 2004), 49. See also 'Glossary: The Tensor', *Libidinal Economy*, xiv-xv.

logos and sense. However, the admittance of difference must not be subsumed by the discourse, as this would re-establish the sovereignty of logos. This is the role of the figural: to guard from the imperialism of the logos. The writing of sense back into thought is accomplished by means of the rediscovery of the figure in the discourse. It is about restoring to the discourse its materiality by showing that a sign cannot fail to be also a figure. The figure within the discourse marks the parallelism of sense and logos. The forgetting of figure in the discourse is a symptom of a way of thinking that claims that the problem of the sign is the problem of representation. If the figure is forgotten it is all to easy to claim that representation is the site of ideological battles without however ever questioning the sovereignty of the logos that lies at the basis of all representation.[5]

One more thing about the figure: it shouldn't be thought of as arbitrary; rather, it is the non-transferable imprint that constitutes the relief and the thickness of the sign. Stripped of the signifying meaning of the sign, the figure is a mark of presence. The figure is a pause, it is the now. While the sign answers to the question "What is happening?" the figure simply asks "Is it happening?"[6] As discourse is inconceivable without pauses, the comma draws attention to its dependence on duration. This is because notions of time and space are conceived from the point of view of the subject who wishes for them to confirm to the measurable and linear logic of the discourse. The most subversive aspect of the pause is that it is both different and inseparable from discourse. But the very notion of difference introduced here knocks reason from its sit of sovereignty and installs undecidability and multiplicity in its place.

By identifying multiplicity, or a folding, within the discourse, Lyotard is able to claim that difference is a quality internal to the sign. According to structuralism difference is expressed as the gap between the discourse (sign) and the object of discourse (referent) ~ note in passing that this is the Hegelian negation (the sign differs from what it is not). The sign and the referent cannot occupy the same place at the same time. Note also that this external difference presumes temporal and spatial linearity and abides by the exclusion principle (Aristotelian logic). For Lyotard difference is not external to the sign, rather it is what makes the sign as the tension between meaning and duration. Difference here does not mean separateness but the condition of collaboration.

---

5. For Louis Althusser representation is the site where ideological wars are being fought: "Ideology is a 'representation' of the Imaginary Relationship of Individuals to their Real conditions of Existence." Louis Althusser, *On Ideology*, (London: New York: Verso, 2008), 36.

6. Jean-François Lyotard, "The Sublime and the Avant-garde." In *The Lyotard Reader*. Edited by, Andrew Benjamin trans Lisa Liebmann, Geoff Bennington and Marian Hobson (Oxford: Blackwell, 1984), 208-11.

Sense is always on the verge of becoming discourse, but discourse always requires something that cannot be explained rationally, yet the Aristotelian-Hegelian formula refuses to acknowledge this debt to the calculus of forces that creates meaning as a relation between parallel entities.

Up to this point it might seem that Lyotard suggests a program for restoring the rights of experience, the sensory spectrum and intuition by recovering their place within discourse. His ultimate goal is however more far-reaching. Through the device of the comma, the title of the book reveals an irreconcilable paradox: The singularity of the pause is guarantied by the identity of logos. The pause / figure can exist as a singularity, as difference and as affect on the condition that this singularity is protected by the sovereignty of the discourse. Lyotard is not trying to replace Discourse with Figure, as doing so would be a reversal ~ yet another logical procedure. Instead he is demonstrating that Discourse has Figure embedded it from the start, and ipso facto that discourse is an undecidable game. Difference therefore is not to be thought outside of Discourse but belonging to it, devoured and sustained by it.

According to this understanding of the figure, images are not representations of an externally given formal reality but are themselves material processes or transmissions of energy. The comma opens the discourse to its outside, to the embodiment in experience. The joining together of "discourse" and "figure" is taking place in perception. Matter appears within discourse as non-mater (comma). The comma acts like a doorstop, it prevents the discourse from closing down on itself, from becoming homogenised. Every comma, every pause, is a manifestation of difference because each and every pause is an embodiment of duration. Yet this wild and untamed difference is often suppressed in favour of the homogeneity of the sign. Comma is the invisible rupture in the discourse, the inarticulate phrase, and the affect-pause that prevents the discourse from shutting down, from collapsing into representation. The comma is not the negation of the discourse but the very element without which the discourse falls apart. Lyotard's strategy in exposing the phenomenological foundation of language is by way of showing that the distance between sign and referent should not be thought of as negation but as a form of expression. Instead of the dialectical relation between the image and the object, Lyotard proposes radical heterogeneity that he names 'thickness' and locates in the first instance in the comma.

Daniel Rubinstein

Tape Plays Teletribunals[1]

Abstract: This paper examines the sexual politics of Richard Linklater's film Tape (2001) in light of Cornelia Vismann's work on legal media and Jacques Derrida's critical revision of confession as a 'machine-event.' I demonstrate how Linklater's Tape manages to avoid obliging the woman to 'playback' too familiar narratives of wounded victimhood, making it both unusual among films' involving a narrative of sexual assault and innovative in thinking the technicity of experience.

Probably we all recognise the vexed relation of woman to allegories of truth or justice. As Cornelia Vismann reminds us 'either 'women' are truth (as allegory) or they betray it.'[2] I am interested in a filmic sub-genre of the displaced tribunal, one that inherits but is not limited to the *Rashomon* effect in which the competing subjective viewpoints nevertheless seem to collude against the plausibility of a female witness.[3] Worse, her lack of plausibility is so habitually woven together with questionable sexuality. My sub-genre concerns sexual assault. Not so much the certificate-challenges of the New French Extreme (?). Rather a selection in which the direction of language sets the stakes. My 'out of court settlements' archive of films include such as Patrick Stettner's *The Business of Strangers* (a CEO and a younger woman who may or may not be on her staff are holed up in a hotel when their flight is cancelled: together they assault a man who the younger woman says is a rapist), Roman Polanski's *Death and the Maiden* (a husband and wife offer shelter to a man stranded in a storm only for the woman ~ to her husband's desperate disavowal ~ to recognise the man's voice and his taste in music as that of the doctor who assaulted her during the reign of a corrupt regime) and Richard Linklater's *Tape* (three former friends reunite some 10 years after high school, only to rake over the events of yesteryear after one of the men extracts a confession from his friend that he had raped the woman that, yes, they both dated). When writing about *Tape* an obvious reference point was Orit Kamir's book *Framed: Women in Law & Film*. Yet while this book spoke to the topic it did not speak to any sense of textuality or problem of media. To get closer to those problems in general for me points to the work of Derrida, but to get to them specifically we have to

1. This paper was presented at *Legal Media: a Colloquium in Memory of Cornelia Vismann*, Birkbeck / Goldsmiths / The Showroom, 10-11 June 2011. This conference is archived on the website of one of its organising bodies at www.forensicarchitecture.org.

Parts of the paper develop my earlier "Wind up: the performative speech acts of *Tape*" *Camera Obscura*, 64, (2007), 112-135.

2. Vismann, Cornelia, "Beyond Image" in *Law, Text, Terror*, Goodrich, Barshack, Schutz, eds. (Abingdon: Glass House Press, 2006), 43.

3. Orit Kamir discusses *Rashomon* at length in her *Framed: Women in Law & Film*, (Durham: Duke University Press, 2006), 43-72.

x
pe
nfession
errida
ony
ent
erformative
letribunals

turn to Cornelia Vismann. The paper today plays back some reflections on *Tape* in light of Vismann's work on the competing interplay of media in the trial and the tribunal.

> 'If television cameras are present in court proceedings, elements that have their origins in the disorder of the tribunal will of necessity seep into the court trial. The ritual of the legal search for justice will give way to the logic of the duel.'[4]

Vismann is writing of the emergence of the televised trial, of the imposition of the order of televisuality and its requisite technologies upon the inherited order of the trial proper. The conceits of the camera take up both space and authority as point-of-view that they were not allotted.

In the case of *Tape*, we do not have a televised trial. Rather we have a film, adapted from Stephen Belber's play of the same name, shot by Richard Linklater over the course of 6 days with then novel digital video (no tape as such). The apparent use of real time ~ 86 minutes restricted to the rudimentary room 19 of the Motor Palace motel ~ is fictitious not only in the sense that the film does not labour to conceal its cuts or its handheld camerawork but also in the sense that the speech-intensive 'action' of this film so rewrites the events of 10 years previously that temporal questions like 'what happened?' and 'when?' become difficult. Often matching the rapid and heated verbal exchanges with its own whip-pan volleys, the camera does not act as dispassionate judge but is involved. By extension, as Vismann notes, the camera teleports a whole other juridical audience into the scene, aligning and realigning identifications.

Given Vismann's combined investigation of law and visual culture, she also remarked on the insertion of cameras into the courtroom in cinema. A crisis is wrought or averted with the aid of the visual evidence supplied by the camera that, with a performative force *par excellence*, never lies. The diegetic insertion of technology as evidence, index, analogy is absent and present in *Tape* in several ways. This is a film in which a man is coerced into confessing a sexual assault that is surreptitiously recorded on tape, and the victim is summoned to receive the gift of apology, which she refuses. More literally legalistic films would not be able to refuse a flashback, would not be able to resist supplying the visual evidence signifying memory. They would restore the missing images, relieve us from the adult anxiety of room 19 and dally in the teenage tensions of a high school graduation party. Is it mere mediumistic

4. Vismann, Cornelia, "Teletribunals: Anatomy of a Medium" in *Grey Room*, 10, (2003), 18.

inheritance that leads tape to refuse the expectation of flashback? No, since *Tape* also sensibly dispenses with the optional prologue and epilogue from Belber's original play. *Tape* refuses to play this game. The task of *Tape* is not to seek out the truth. Rather *Tape* stakes out the only too familiar trope of the exchange of women between men and were Amy to show and tell (executed cinematically as flashback) this would only pander to her place in their story. Whether victim or not, the one thing she is, is 'hot.' While some online reviews persist in misreading the narrative of *Tape* as one about two friends, with the woman already sequestered within their script, it is one of the strengths of the film that, through the making of a tape-recording, the trope of gender is exposed and not consolidated. It is not only that the displaced tribunal of *Tape* ironizes the trial and delivers a witty reversal of a 'dumb guy and smart guy' routine in so doing. Rather, it is the unexpected participation of the woman who blanks the script written for her as evidence or trophy or other object (a cassette tape even), and rather sends the legalistic performatives of the film into overdrive. Jon's technical mediation in *Tape* is also at stake, not through visual flashback but through audio playback.

For it is a cassette tape, rather than a camera, that is embedded within this film as the index of its archive fever. Upfront, the film's title *Tape* takes an aspirational centre stage; unravelling magnetic tape is suggested as the titles snake across the screen bracketing the film; a cheap cassette circulates from hand to hand within the narrative. This cassette *might* be a legal object ~ it does contain what appears to be the confession of a sexual assault never previously brought to justice. Yet Vince, who engineers the production of this tape, barely refers to it as something that might enter a legal environment other than the effective tribunal of room 19 of the Motor Palace. The tape, it seems, is not for the record. The two named trajectories for the tape are, firstly, that it could be given to Amy who might be 'interested' to hear its contents ~ this before the pair realise that Amy is now an Assistant District Attorney, and secondly that this might spark the beginning of Vince's own movie career. Like the more socially-mobile Jon, who is screening his first film at the Lansing Film Festival ~ the ostensible occasion for this school reunion ~ Vince too might use art to transcend his life, to learn from his mistakes, and make something *meaningful*.

Unlike a flashback that is used to convey memory, that is memory as cinematically configured according to a very narrow prescription of a reel that can more or less simply be rewound and replayed, in this temporally concentrated motel room, we see Vince manufacture the tape. It is quite the production. Though we learn that the subject of Amy always comes up whenever these two guys get together, this time, under the makeshift interrogation lights of Room 19, Vince will not let Jon off the hook and, in the manner of a belligerent prosecution, needles Jon into revealing 'what happened' that night at the party after graduation. We should note that the conversation between the two of them has already set up the question of violence; of what merely amounts to a 'threatening appearance' and of what might constitute violence as such, and articulated in similar terms, whether one of them merely 'acts in a phallic fashion' or actually *is* 'a dick'. Jon's subsequent contorted concession that he applied 'excessive linguistic pressure' as the means with which to coerce Amy into having sex with him might be easily caricatured by Vince as 'bullshit,' but it is not the suggestion that the language of force is either the prequel to or the mask of violence in the world that is most interesting, rather it is that language is not signification alone but also force.

Writing of the discrepant methods used by Michel Foucault and Pierre Legendre in their treatment of the trials of Pierre Rivière and Corporal Lortie respectively, Vismann pays attention to their understanding of the relation between writing, especially written confession and the deed of murder. In the case of Foucault, Rivière's belated statement is yet understood by Foucault as predictive of his crime. Vismann writes that 'Speech acts reveal their tragic dimension [...]. Once let loose, they cannot be stopped in their tracks.'[5] What is compelling about *Tape* is that while speech acts are indeed let loose and cannot in a sense be stopped, their tracks are not analogue, reference to 'tape' notwithstanding. They do not simply or irrefutably betray the one who made them, pointing them out. In spite of technology's promise to capture that which it records ~ and the perfect copy made by the low-end Walmart tape recorder hidden in a bag under a table on the other side of the room gives the lie to this fantasy ~ every track remains beholden to the countersignature of the other. I'll come to Amy's devastating response to the trap in which she manages not to be set soon. First I will address the complex character of Jon's confession and the concomitant stream of apologies by way of Vismann's critical presentation of Legendre as well as Derrida's attention to the performative genre of *Confessions*.

For Foucault as there would be for Derrida, there are multiple procedures of truthfinding at stake in a trial, which may 'found' rather than simply 'find' that which they seek. For Legendre attention is more narrowly focused upon the field of language, a field construed as having been wounded by a deed without a word, a crime without an accompanying sentence: this wound must be redressed by the court proceedings; the court must enjoin the accused to refer to the crime in the first person ('I killed X...'). The restitution effected by the use of the first person is towards that of the institution of language.

---

5. Vismann, Cornelia, "*Rejouer les Crimes* Theatre vs Video" in *Cardozo Studies in Law & Literature*, 11:2. (1999), 165.

Every trial addresses itself to this larger criteria through the sentence that the defendant must utter in the first person, thus the stakes always point beyond the individual crime. They point towards a 'cure for the office of the father' as Vismann says, suggesting that a paternal metaphor of language is at stake.[6]

If we do not have 'missing images' supplied by *Tape*, if we cannot see 'then,' we have instead yet more words (*Tape* is already verbose). The forging of the tape produces an aural slippage in the otherwise visually consistent room: it is only played back once for verification, immediately after Jon eventually and crudely shouts, in the first person, that he 'pinned her arms back and stuck [his] dick in.' In Legendre's terms, as presented by Vismann, we have a result. The tape repeats the most incriminating sentence; Jon is later to say, under pressure from Amy as to why he suddenly 10 years later wants to apologise, that after hearing what he said on the tape, what he did 'hit him' and he wanted to say that he was sorry. Not during the event, not during the confession, but on hearing himself speak on tape, Jon is struck by his own deed.

Jon is also wounded in the heat of the exchange with Vince, not so much because he has now spoken about that night at the party, but because Vince so wound him up as to make him talk of it, and on tape too. His authority is in question, and Jon is the film-maker here. While *Tape* resists the temptation to have the outraged Jon literally complain of Vince *taping* him without consent, the association is in the air, and this between two men, one or more of who may be a dick.[7] I say this not just to be contentious or flippant, but because I think the film is highly conscious of the phonetic and typographic similarity between the two words, tape and rape. Tape: an archival medium that should faithfully store the contents it captures. I've suggested already that the cheapness of Vince's tape, not to mention its now antique status in the history of technology, and our generation's memory of the ready fallibility of such media, suggest the reverse. But the problem is not simply that storage media might fall apart, be literally divisible, although it might. Rather the supplement that the recording donates to that which is recorded always reinscribes the event and does not simply re-present it. As Derrida writes, 'the archive produces the event no less than it records or consigns it.'[8] Likewise, rape as a meaningful inscription loses ground. In the singular case of this film, Jon's actions, as well as his speech, are vulnerable to the countersignature of the other. Thus, in the face of Jon's effusive, near endless, apologies, Amy says she was not raped. Again, while nervous laughter is prompted on numerous

6. Vismann, "*Rejouer*" 167.

7. NB. 'dick' as colloquial for detective.

8. Derrida, "Typewriter Ribbon: Limited Ink II" in *Without Alibi*, (Stanford: Stanford University Press, 2002), 101.

occasions, the film is not at all facetious about this subject matter, neither does it remove or belittle the criminality of sexual assault.

Rather than introduce Amy ~ the last one of the three to arrive at the Motor Palace ~ as the final witness to and guarantee of this rape narrative, *Tape* changes tack. *Tape* the film and the Walmart cassette part company. Rather than remain the ruse through which the relation between Jon and Vince is held in place, Amy undoes their authority. Rather than simply refuse the apology because she says she was not raped, Amy structurally recodes it as a speech act that does not have her as its object or the intention to apologise as its aim.

Putting pressure on what is called apology, Amy's effective re-write brings out Jon's uncanny repetition of the genre of *Confessions* as diagnosed by Paul de Man and by Derrida.[9] There should be no trace of repetition in such a thing as confession. De Man elaborates problems with the performative capacity of confession through Rousseau who, in writings 10 years apart, confesses to the same event twice (that event, famously, being putting the blame for the theft of a ribbon that Rousseau himself had stolen onto a convenient servant girl, Marion). De Man plots out these two instances, from Rousseau's *Reveries* as well as the eponymous *Confessions*, such that the first registers as the confession of an event and the second as the machinic making of an excuse. The sinister insinuation of the latter manifests in the transference of the guilt from committing an offence, to the guilty pleasure in writing about it.

Throwing out of court Jon's professed sincerity of apology, Amy counters: 'You didn't like what you said on the tape Jon, so you came back to say it little more eloquently.' As with Rousseau, the apology serves only to prolong Jon's airtime and to broadcast his guilt. For while it required substantial goading for Vince to sufficiently wind Jon up until his confession bursts out, once started, he can barely stop. He really is sorry! Truly. Genuinely. Sincerely. This windbag apologises something like 9 times, not to mention those uttered 'in general' before Amy arrives.

Without detailing the breadth of Derrida's intervention here, suffice to say he pulls De Man up for apparently forgetting that Rousseau is already in a state of repetition in his curious structural duplication of the confession of a minor crime as pivotal moment in that other inaugural work, Augustine's *Confessions*. Moreover, Derrida finds De Man overly close to a duplication of the separation of constative from performative when he separates event of confession (in the first instance) to the machine of excuse or apology (in the second or any other instance). While event is traditionally conceived as spontaneous, affective

9. See Derrida, "Typewriter Ribbon," and Paul de Man "Excuses (*Confessions*)" in *Allegories of Reading*, (New Haven & London: Yale University Press, 1979), 278-301.

and organic and while the mechanical is thought of as repetitious, unfeeling, automata, Derrida comes to hyphenate the two. He recasts the performative that holds out so much temptation for the spontaneous, as machine-event.[10] The perversion that is pleasure in writing is there from the 'first'. 'First' like 'when' in the belated relays of *Tape*, is difficult to determine, and the archives of the confession are, as Derrida remarks, 'interminable'.[11] Thus speech acts cannot be stopped, not because they command unerring precision, but because their course can always be redirected...

These remarks echo those of Vismann in her conclusion to the essay on the question of 'replaying the crime' ('*Rejouer les Crimes*'). There, instead of magnifying a fear of media and calling a halt to the intercession of images in the name of the judge, Vismann points to the 'play of gazes' in the theatre of justice as already themselves citational ~ the machinic quality to which reprographic media draw attention and which De Man framed as secondary.[12] Citationality, in all senses, is exploited by Amy. It is not that only Amy constitutively can have the last word ~ and a last word that she explicitly denies to Jon ~ but rather that the force of surprise is so much on her side that neither man knows how to continue.

Amy derails the authority of Jon's actions as his apology retroactively positions them by saying that she was not raped, ruining the first person affirmation of his linguistic reparation. Jon may well have been 'reckless' as to Amy's consent that night ~ and it comes as another shock for him to learn that she was then in love with him.[13]Putting his hand over her mouth certainly contributed to the lack of any accompanying speech on her part that night. But speaking now in room 19, Amy rewrites the place where she is expected to be as the passively functioning tape recording the inscriptions of the men. *Tape* decks the twin clichés of gender and technology ~ of inscription as phallic mark on virgin ground, and of passive feminine sexuality as inaugurated in reaction to the active 'writing' of masculine sexuality. In this light, Jon's insistence that he really means what he says and his pleas for Amy to accept his apologies function as another attempted insemination.

Now Amy's rewrite is not easy. Twice more she demonstrates her distance from their plot. Firstly, she lets rip a stream of lurid invective at Jon wishing a brutal assault upon his person, only to abruptly shift with disarming irony

---

10. In this light we might think of the implications of the name of the Motor Palace.

11. Derrida, "Typewriter Ribbon", 71.

12. Vismann, "*Rejouer les Crimes*", 174.

13. Legal scholar Ngaire Naffine notes both that the UK Sexual Offences Act includes the codicil that a man may be judged guilty of rape if he is 'reckless' as to whether the woman consents (21, n.67), and that in Australian legislation the Victorian Parliament includes silence on the part of the woman as 'enough to show that the act took place without that person's free agreement' (37). See her "Possession: Erotic Love in the Law of Rape" in *The Modern Law Review*, 57:1, (1994), 10-37.

into a smile, charging the men with having prescribed just such a performance. As they reel she delivers another blow. Mobilising the language of the law, she fakes a phone call to the police and appears to shop both Jon and Vince, the first for a 'verified' Criminal Sexual Conduct felony and the second for possession of illegal substances. Unable to marshall further apologies to a body for whom they cut no ice, Jon hands himself over to the judgement of the other. Meanwhile, Vince in panic flushes his drugs and destroys the tape he had so laboured to make. Revealing the hoax, Amy leaves the room, leaves *Tape*, and leaves the men without their alibi, both in the end the 'dumb guy'.

Remarkable extradiegetically as it is that Robert Sean Leonard [Jon] in a cast interview still refers to *Tape* in comparison to *Rashomon* as if we end this film unable to decide between the testimonies of the two witnesses, and, that several years after the release of *Tape*, Uma Thurman was to front a number of execrable Virgin Media advertisements in which she personified exactly the kind of domesticated media that is deconstructed in *Tape*, *Tape* nevertheless displays the 'ordeal' of the decision, on which Vismann was to insist in her seminars on Derrida's 'Force of Law' at Goldsmiths.[14] It is not that Amy becomes identical with justice, fully present at such. The calls she makes, as I've suggested are shot through with citational precedent, yet her audience do not see this machine event coming.

Lynn Turner

---

14. Derrida, Jacques, "Force of Law" in Cornell, Drucilla et al eds. *Deconstruction & the Possibility of Justice*, (New York & London: Routledge, 1992), 24. I very much appreciated Cornelia's kindness and brilliance in contributing seminars on "Force of Law" for the MA class on performativity that I was teaching in 2006 during her time as Visiting Leverhulme Professor at Goldsmiths and Birkbeck.

Becoming Gay:

Deleuze, Feminism and Queer Theory[1]

Abstract: In my contribution I want to address some of the texts by Gilles Deleuze and Felix Guattari (henceforth: D|G*) and investigate their relationship to feminist theory. I would also like to make some suggestions concerning a possible theoretical development consisting of a queering of* D|G*'s positions. My critical reading of Deleuze is directed against some views taken by Judith Butler, not because I think her work is "too poststructuralist" or "too constructivist", but because it is not poststructuralist and constructivist enough. My presentation also aims at a rematerialisation of the body, of gender and of sexuality, as it has been demanded by a growing number of scholars in recent times. Deleuzian concepts like "becoming woman" are located at the centre of this rematerialisation. A critical analysis of desire, as it is used by the authors of* Anti-Oedipus *and* Thousand Plateaus, *is crucial in order to think productively about a queering of* D|G.

Freudian Desire and Queer Criticism

In 1972, Guy Hocquenghem, gay revolutionary activist and writer, published his manifesto, *Le désir homosexuel*, followed by another text, entitled *L'après-mai des faunes*. Both texts address the open persecution of homosexuals by the French state, but also talk about the homophobic paranoia of French society, which made homosexuals prisoners of heteronormative concepts of sexuality. In France, homosexuality was perceived either as a crime to be kept in check by the police and the courts or as a psychological abnormality that should be treated. An important part of his analysis of the homosexual condition of his time was an assault on Sigmund Freud and his school, and especially on Freud's concept of desire and its further development by Jacques Lacan. Freudianism ~ according to Hocquenghem ~ maintains a privileged position, because it is both the discoverer of the mechanisms of desire and the institution of its control.[2] Control is exercised by the inscription of homosexual energy (force) into the oedipal triangle, which is at the center of psychoanalysis and the linchpin of western culture.[3] One thing is certain,

1. I owe the title of this paper to Didier Eribon, *Réflexions sur la question gay* (Paris: Fayard, 1999), 456.

2. "Le freudisme joue un rôle privilégié : il est à la fois le découvreur des mécanismes du désir et l'organisme de leur contrôle." Guy Hocquenghem, *Homosexual Desire*, trans Daniella Dangoor (London: Allison & Busby, 1978), 59. See also: Lawrence R. Schehr, "Defense and Illustration of Gay Liberation," *Yale French Studies* 90 (1996): 139-152, 140 f.

3. "At a time when capitalist individualisation is undermining the family by depriving it of its essential functions, the Oedipus complex represents the internalisation of the family institution [...] This is only proper: the Oedipus complex is the only effective means of controlling the libido. Stages

ender
ne body
xuality
minism
ueer theory
ay liberation
materialization
oststructural
eleuze and Guattari

if we believe the Freudians: homosexuals cannot escape their dominant, domineering and loving mothers. Did not Marcel Proust rewrite the diabolical passages in 'A la recherche du temps perdu' only after his mother's death? According to Hocquenghem, the desire to maternalise ("materniser") everything integrated homosexuals into the infernal oedipal ballet, assigning him the role of the damned in the process. This way, Freudianism was able to identify both the cause and the person responsible for homosexuality. As important as their libido is for the feelings of human beings, it is entangled in the oedipal privatization from which there is no getaway for homosexuals. In the seventies this fundamental discovery of the Freudian school had solidified discursively and even renowned French mass media started mother-bashing when it came to explanations of homosexuality.

The astounding certainties provided by the Freudians not only secured the control mechanisms of homosexualities within the oedipal triangle, but included homosexuals also within a tyrannical dichotomy of active and passive. Every homosexual subject is called upon defining his sexual identity in relation to activism or passivism. The therapeutic drive is clearly focused on the allegedly passive homosexuals. Therapists define the character of the homosexual by looking through the lens of pathologic passivity. Passive homosexuals ~ according to the popularized version of Freudian theory ~ share hysteria and an unbalanced personality with women. Both, women and passive homosexuals, lack the phallus and the phallus is the only possible allocator of identity. Within the dominant discourse, the true, i.e. passive homosexual is nothing but an ersatz woman, an illusion of woman, a copy of woman. Homosexuals lack essence; it is a desperate void that characterizes / designates homosexuals. This emptiness can be filled to some extent by sublimation, i.e. through art or the creation of cultural artefacts / objects. Since homosexuality is a form of emptiness, death equals homosexual desire, if not real death, then at least symbolical death.

The introduction for Hocquenghem's acerbic analysis of the homophobic structure in Freudian thought was written by Gilles Deleuze, who was very much inspired by the young gay author, especially by his critique of the oedipal triangle, the 'restricted Trinitarian formula ~ oedipal, neurotic: papa ~ mama ~ me'.[4] Deleuze, who published his monumental *Anti-Oedipus* with Felix Guattari in 1972, addressed the concept of desire in his foreword to Hocquenghem's volume:

---

need to be built, a pyramidal construction that will enclose homosexual desire within the three sides of the triangle." Hocquenghem, *Homosexual Desire*, 60; 65.

4. Gilles Deleuze and Félix Guattari, *Anti-Ödipus: Kapitalismus und Schizophrenie I* (Frankfurt / Main: Syndikat, 1986), 32 [my translation, N.F.].

> "Some of the more ridiculous pages Freud ever wrote are those on "fellatio": such a bizarre and "shocking" desire can have no worth of its own; it must be traceable to a cow udder, and from there to the mother's breast. Freud thinks we would get more pleasure sucking on a cow udder. Interpret, regress, push toward regression. It just makes Hocquenghem laugh.[5]

Deleuze continues:

> "It is not the past but the present that determines whether one is homosexual, once we admit that childhood was already a presence that did not refer to a past. Because desire never represents anything, and it doesn't refer back to something waiting in the wings of the familial or personal theatre. Desire makes connections, it assembles, it machines."[6]

"Becoming Woman"

D|G's thoughts and writing affect the topic at hand in a twofold way: First there is the line of flight of the "becoming woman", a concept that was rather misunderstood and criticized than understood and accepted. D|G introduce this concept extensively in the tenth chapter of 'A *Thousand Plateaus*', which is entitled 'Becoming Intense, Becoming Animal, Becoming Imperceptible'.[7] As can be seen from the chapter's title, it revolves around the crucial notion of the becoming, a concept that is diametrically opposed to the essentialist notion of the essence. D|G explain becoming by what it is not, at first.

> "A becoming is not a correspondence between relations. But neither is it a resemblance, an imitation, or, at the limit, an identification. [...] To become is not to progress or regress along a series. Above all, becoming does not occur in the imagination, even when the imagination reaches the highest cosmic or dynamic level [...]. Becoming-animal are neither dreams nor fantasies. They are perfectly real. But what reality is at issue here? For if becoming animal does not

5. Gilles Deleuze, "Vorwort zu L'après-mai des faunes," in Gilles Deleuze, *Die einsame Insel: Texte und Gesprä-che* 1953-1974 (Frankfurt / Main: Suhrkamp, 2003), 412-418, 413.

6. Deleuze, "Vorwort zu L'après-mai des faunes," 413.

7. Gilles Deleuze and Félix Guattari, *Tausend Plateaus: Kapitalismus und Schizophrenie* (Berlin: Merve, 1997), 317-422.

consist in playing animal or imitating an animal, it is clear that the human being does not really become an animal any more than the animal "really" becomes something else. Becoming produces nothing other than itself. We fall into a false alternative if we say that you either imitate or you are.[8] [...] Becoming can and should be qualified as becoming-animal in the absence of a term that would be the animal become."[9]

And much later, in the same chapter, D|G ramble on:

> "Becoming animal is only one becoming among others. A kind of order or apparent progression can be established for the segments of becoming in which we find ourselves; becoming-woman, becoming-child; becoming animal, vegetable, or ~ mineral; becomings-molecular of all kinds, becoming particles. [...] Singing or composing, painting, writing have no other aim: to unleash these becomings. Especially music; music is traversed by a becoming-woman, becoming-child, [...]"[10]

I want to emphasize D|G's observation that this *Great Chain of Becoming* only seemingly represents a progress from different segments of becoming. Music and writing for example cannot be placed into a definite stage of future progress.[11] I will come back to this point later on.

On the same page, D|G attempt a positive definition of becoming:

> "Starting from the form one has, the subject one is, the organs one has, or the functions one fulfills, becoming is to extract particles between which one establishes the relations of movement and rest, speed and slowness that are closest to what is becoming, and through which one becomes. This is the sense in which becoming is the process of desire."[12]

---

8. Deleuze and Guattari, *A Thousand Plateaus. Capitalism and Schizophrenia* (Minneapolis, MN: University of Minnesota Press, 1987), 262.

9. Deleuze and Guattari, *A Thousand Plateaus*, 262.

10. Deleuze and Guattari, *A Thousand Plateaus*, 300.

11. "Futurus" is the PFA of the Latin verb fieri which means "to become".

12. Deleuze and Guattari, *A Thousand Plateaus*, 300-301.

D|G differentiate between molar and molecular forms of subjects: The subject for D|G is the result of diverse force relations that constantly shape and shift its form. [D|G] call these two different states "molar" and "molecular": molar means rigid, fixed and bulk headed sedimentations, whereas molecular denotes flexibility, liquidity, mobility and undecidability. The individual always moves between these two states, between being and becoming something other.[13] The concept of becoming-woman is a contested and debated one. If one looks close enough at the text, however, the misunderstandings dissolve sooner or later. Since 'all becomings are molecular', D|G underscore the fact that there is 'a becoming-woman, a becoming-child, that do not resemble the woman or the child as clearly distinct molar entities [...] Becoming woman is not imitating [the molar entity] or even transforming oneself into it.' Becoming-woman consists of 'emitting particles that enter the relation of movement and rest, or the zone of proximity, of a microfeminity, in other words, that produce in us a molecular woman, create the molecular woman.'[14] And in concluding the round dance of quotations: 'Although all becomings are already molecular, including becoming-woman, it must be said that all becomings begin with and pass through becoming-woman. It is the key to all other becomings.'[15] "Why are there so many becomings of man, but no becoming-man? First because man is majoritarian par excellence, whereas becomings are minoritarian; all becoming is a becoming-minoritarian. [...] Even Blacks, as the Black Panthers said, must become-black."[16] The opposition minoritarian ~ majoritarian is not a mathematical relation: "Majority implies a constant, of expression or content, serving as a standard measure by which to evaluate it." This constant is "the average adult-white-heterosexual-european-male speaking a standard language [...] even if he is less numerous than the mosquitoes, children, women, blacks, peasants, homosexuals, etc."[17]

In a conversation with Claire Parnet Deleuze explained the majoritarian man: "The adult male has no becoming. He may become woman, if he participates in minoritarian processes."[18] 'Becoming-woman' is the act or the practice of embodying of female instability and multiplicity, the resistance

13. "Postsexuelle Körper," http://www.medienkunstnetz.de/themen/cyborg_bodies/postsexuelle_koerper/11/, accessed 21.01.08 [my translation, N.F.].

14. Deleuze and Guattari, *A Thousand Plateaus*, 303-304.

15. Deleuze and Guattari, *A Thousand Plateaus*, 306.

16. Deleuze and Guattari, *A Thousand Plateaus*, 320-321.

17. Deleuze and Guattari, *A Thousand Plateaus*, 116.

18. "L'homme mâle adulte, il n'a pas un devenir. Il peut devenir femme, alors il s'engage dans les processus mino-ritaires. La gauche, c'est l'ensemble des processus de devenir minoritaires. Donc, je peux dire, à la lettre: la ma-jorité c'est personne, la minorité c'est tout le monde. C'est ça, être de gauche : savoir que la minorité, c'est tout le monde." Gilles Deleuze and Claire Parnet, *L'Abécédiaire de Gilles Deleuze* (Paris, 1996), video edition [my translation, N.F.].

against the status of the solid and the representative which is defined as male. Brian Massumi describes becoming as a dispersed outside, as 'the great dissipative outside stretching uncertainly on the wild side of the welcome mat'.[19] Becoming woman therefore is a necessary state in the process of becoming, even if Massumi concedes, that the wording by D|G is sexist.[20] "The feminine gender stereotype involves greater indeterminacy ('fickle') and movement ('flighty') and has been burdened by the patriarchal tradition with a disproportionate load of paradox (virgin / whore, mother / lover)".[21]

These are, arguably, the most important positions taken by D|G with regard to becomimg-woman. They have been severely criticized by feminists. While feminist thinkers like Rosi Braidotti, Claire Colebrook, Elizabeth Grosz and others have attempted to connect D|G to feminist theory in order to develop a non-identitary definition of corporeality, there is probably no greater chasm in feminist thinking than between adherents of a Deleuzian concept of the body and Judith Butler. Butler's implicit insistence on an opposition between sex and gender abolished the dualism between body and mind on the one hand, while preserving it on the other. By arguing that the so-called natural body is always already part of a discourse, she reduces every reference to the natural body to a discursive effect.[22] "Accordingly, the attempt is made to 'free' gender from sex ~ to see gender not as cultural overlay of sex but as that which produces 'sex' as a discursive given [...] Gender is not, then, the social construction of 'sex'; 'sex' is yet one more discursive effect." Any form of a pre-discursive outside is therefore cast aside. Although for Butler the body is a material body, this materiality is only existent within discourse and does not include a material raw form. Corporeality cannot be conceived of outside of discourse. "[...] Butler argues that corporeality may not be discursive [...] but this status as prediscursive is an effect of discourse."[23] According to Butler, any form of imagining the body as a given outside object would lead invariably to a biologist determinism. This assertion rests on the definition of representation in Butler's work: Representation for Butler consists of a negation of materiality: "To posit a materiality outside of language is still to posit that materiality,

---

19. Brian Massumi, *A User's Guide to Capitalism and Schizophrenia: Deviations from Deleuze and Guattari* (Cambridge, MA: MIT Press, 1992), 95.

20. "Deleuze and Guattari's formulation of the concept of "becoming-woman" is indeed sexist. The burden of change is placed on women, since it is their cliché that is singled out." Massumi, *A User's Guide*, 89.

21. Massumi, *A User's Guide*, 86.

22. Abigail Bray and Claire Colebrook, "The Haunted Flesh: Corporeal Feminism and the Politics of (Dis)Embodiment," *Signs* vol. 24, no. 1 (Autumn, 1998): 35-67, 42. The authors refer to Judith Butler, *Bodies That Matter: On the Discursive Limits of Sex* (New York: Routledge, 1993), 22.

23. Bray and Colebrook, "The Haunted Flesh," 42. Butler, *Bodies That Matter*, 30. In the German translation the quotation is found on page 32f.

and that materiality so posited will retain that positing as its constitutive condition."[24] Abigail Bray and Claire Colebrook use this conception of representation as a departure for a critique of Butler: The harsh separation between representation and matter extends the Western Cartesian dualism and thus puts an end to debates about specific problems like eating disorders. "Eating disorders, for example, might not possess a single relation to representation, nor could they be exhaustively accounted for through some general theory of signification and its relation to the signified."[25] One could transcend the critique by Bray and Colebrook by asking what kind of matter Butler talks about when she insists that materializations always constitute a stabilization, "to produce the effect of boundary, fixity, and surface we call matter"?[26] I would polemically call this definition of matter a Newtonian, pre-thermodynamical essentialism that ignores the existence of fluid and gassy matter. This misconception of matter is enhanced by Butler's insistence on the concept of sedimentation, i.e. residue of solid matter in different layers. Matter for Butler is a problem of solid body physics.[27]

> "It is still not acceptable for the flesh and boundaries of fluid, volatile, messy, leaky bodies to be included in [philosophical] discourse. [...] When [philosophers] speak of the body they still often fail to talk about a body that breaks its boundaries ~ urinates, bleeds, vomits, farts, engulfs tampons, objects of sexual desire, ejaculates and gives birth."[28]

Sedimentation without the defining influence of water and wind, however, is inconceivable. Currents, erosion, and the various shifting of the ground have a material power in the creation of sediments.[29] Even if one wants to limit matter

---

24. Butler, *Bodies That Matter*, 67-68.

25. Bray and Colebrook, "The Haunted Flesh," 43.

26. Butler, *Bodies That Matter*, 9.

27. Solid body physics pretty much remains a domain of male physicists. Margaret W. Rossiter, "Which Science? Which Women?," *Osiris*, vol. 12, Women, Gender, and Science: New Directions. (1997): 169-185, 174.

28. Robyn Longhurst, *Bodies: Exploring Fluid Boundaries* (London: Routledge, 2001), 223. Longhurst speaks about geographical discourses only and I have to confess that I alienated her quotation from its context in order to make a point about philosophy. This quote reads almost like D|G's famous quotation in *Anti-Oedipus*: "It is at work everywhere [... it] breathes, it heats, it eats. It shits and fucks." Deleuze and Guattari, *Anti-Oedipus*, 1.

29. Lawrence P. Sanford, "New Sedimentation, Resuspension, and Burial," *Limnology and Oceanography* vol. 37, no. 6. (Sep. 1992): 1164-1178. John McManus, "Temporal and Spatial Variations in Estuarine Sedimentation," *Estuaries* vol. 21, no. 4, Part A: Dedicated Issue: Transport, Retention, Transformation Processes and Their Bio-logical Control in Estuarine and Coastal Systems: Second International Joint Conference, Estuarine and Coastal Sciences Association and Estuarine Research

to solid bodies "to produce the effect of boundary, fixity, and surface we call matter" there are forces at work that can only be described in the etiology of becoming. Sedimentation requires by definition a force outside of the bodies that become layered sediments. "[...] by arguing that matter, while not purely discursive, is still other than discursive, Butler sustains an opposition between discourse and some, outside [...]"[30]

If we look at the Deleuzian concept of strata and layers, we discover a much more supple definition. A sedimentation, once it is achieved, is not fixed but almost fluid.

> "[...] there is no reason to think that all matter is confined to the physicochemical strata: there exists a submolecular, unformed Matter. Similarly, not all Life is confined to the organic strata: rather, the organism is that which life sets against itself in order to limit itself, and there is a life all the more intense, all the more powerful for being anorganic."[31]

Elizabeth Grosz has taken up the idea of fluid and malleable matter in her collection of essays entitled *Space, Time and Perversion* (1995). According to her, the border between the inside and the outside cannot be drawn sharply but diffuse as pliable, fluid, and dynamic. Thus the border between the Self and the Other that is so constitutive for representation is exposed to a constant process of refiguration and negotiation.[32] Deleuze, in explaining Foucault's work, provided a formula that is even more penetrating: "The Outside is not a fixed limit but moving matter animated by peristaltic movements, folds and foldings that altogether make up an inside: they are not something other than the outside, but precisely the inside *of* an outside."[33] Where Butler's model of performativity rests on the assumption of a materialization of the corporeal through repetition as sediments, Grosz insisted on the body's and sexuality's instability.[34] According to her, bodies have to be conceived of as entities that can do more than society / culture acknowledge. Here we have a body with

---

Federation. (Dec. 1998): 622-634.

30. Bray and Colebrook, "The Haunted Flesh," 43.

31. Deleuze and Guattari, *A Thousand Plateaus*, 554.

32. Elizabeth Grozs, *Space, Time and Perversion: Essays on the Politics of Bodies* (New York: Routledge, 1995). See also Linda Martín Alcoff, "Philosophy Matters: A Review of Recent Works in Feminist Philosophy," *Signs* vol. 25, no. 3 (Spring, 2000): 841-882, 860-868.

33. Deleuze, *Foucault* (Minneapolis, MN: University of Minnesota Press, 1988), 97.

34. Elizabeth Grozs, "Experimental Desire. Rethinking Queer Subjectivity," in *Supposing the Subject*, ed. Joan Copjec (London, New York: Verso, 1994), 133-157.

extremely fluid borders, with the ability to cough up the interior and to incorporate the exterior.

Let's move back from Butler and Grosz to D|G: For some feminists, the concept of becoming-woman is just another example for the (all-too) well-known process of female exclusion from representation by presenting this exclusion as the result of dissolution of representation. Luce Irigaray and Alice Jardine have argued that even if Deleuzian thinking is understood as innovative it contained an implicit rejection of femininity. Irigaray expressed strong reservations against the Deleuzian project, "arguing that fluidity, non-being, liminality and marginality, as well as a condition of symbolic exile are part and parcel of women's history of oppression."[35] One could sum up Irigaray's und Jardine's line of reasoning in one question: Does not 'becoming-woman' risk to repeat the historical invisibility of women in the name of a literary and philosophical experiment by scraping out an indispensable category and by celebrating its disappearance? According to Jardine, in reference to animated materiality the concept of becoming turns women into simulacra, "a female figure caught in a whirling sea of male configurations".[36] Rosi Braidotti, who identifies herself as a Deleuzian feminist and has fought for a feminist reinterpretation of D|G, concluded in 1994 "[...] no other specificity is granted to women's struggles and discursivity: the highly specific theoretical and political itineraries of feminism are thus reduced to a generalised contribution to the final destruction of the knowing subject."[37] It is important to note, however, that Braidotti does not refer to D|G's major texts, but to a small article by Guattari and to the queer activist Hocquenghem, writing about the destruction of sexuality.[38] This casualness is telling, since D|G write in *A Thousand Plateaus* about the indispensability of feminism: "It is, of course, indispensable for women to conduct a molar politics, with a view of winning back their own organism, their own history, their own subjectivity: 'we as women...' makes its appearance as a subject of enunciation."[39]

Be that as it may, Braidotti seems to have shifted her position, because she noted an honest attempt at undermining the oedipal order by the concept of becoming. On the other hand she indicts D|G for taking the position of the, 'I know, but':

---

35. Rosi Braidotti, "Nomadism with a Difference: Deleuze's Legacy in a Feminist Perspective," *Man and World*, 29 (1996): 305-314, 310.

36. Alice A. Jardine, *Gynesis: Configurations of Woman and Modernity* (Ithaca, NY: Cornell University Press, 1985), 217.

37. Rosi Braidotti, "Patterns of Dissonance: Women and / in Philosophy," in *Feministische Philosophie*, ed. Herta Nagl-Docekal (Wien: R. Oldenbourg, 1990), 108-122, 117.

38. Braidotti, "Patterns of Dissonance," fn 11.

39. Deleuze and Guattari, *A Thousand Plateaus*, 304.

> "[...It] seems to me that Deleuze's theory of becoming is obviously determined by his location as an embodied male subject for whom the dissolution of identities based on the phallus results in by-passing gender altogether, toward a multiple sexuality. This, however, may not be the option best suited to female embodied subjects."[40]

Even if D|G's position as molar men is not the best starting point for a feminist critique, Braidotti grants D|G that by abolishing the masculinist foundations of classical subjectivity they open up new potentials for feminist empowerment.[41] The emphasis on thinking differently with the insistence on the de-essentializing of the body, of sexuality and sexual identity contains, according to Braidotti, the possibility of constructing of new desiring subjects.[42] "We need to learn how to think differently, especially about our own notion of the subject; this is one of the points where the Deleuzian project intersects with feminist theory."[43]

Desire as Lack

Insofar as one wants to follow Judith Butler in her sympathetic attempt to de-essentialize the body and gender, for a deluded Deleuzian problems arise when Butler uses Lacanian psychoanalysis in order to clarify the corporeal foundations of subjectivity. Lacan's theory of the imaginary is founded on the observation of the mirror stage in child development, the period between the 6th and the 18th month of life, when a child starts to recognize itself in front of a mirror. This self-identificatory act alters the perception of the self, in a way it is the precondition for the perception of the self: the partial objects of the body are never perceived as a totality; it is only the gaze from outside that shows the child as a complete body. According to Lacan, this mirror stages coincides with the birth of the Ego. On the other side, it constitutes the beginning of alienation, because in the mirror stage the child observes a corporeal unity that it does not feel. The child therefore identifies with something that it is not, i.e. with the 'total form of the body' in a location it

---

40. Rosi Braidotti, *Nomadic Subjects: Embodiment and Sexual Difference in Contemporary Feminist Theory* (New York: Columbia University Press, 1994), 122.

41. Braidotti, Nomadic Subjects, 149.

42. Rosi Braidotti, "Toward a New Nomadism: Feminist Deleuzean Tracks; or, Metaphysics and Metabolism," in *Gilles Deleuze and the Theater of Philosophy*, eds. Constantin V. Boundas and Dorothea Olkowski (New York: Routeledge, 1994), 159-185, 163. See also Kimberly Lamm, "Writing Becoming-Woman: The Movement of Deleuzean Thought in Contemporary American Poetry," in *theory@buffalo* 8, http://wings.buffalo.edu/theory/archive/archive.html, accessed January 19, 2008.

43. Rosi Braidotti, "Nomadism with a Difference," 305-314, 308.

does not inhabit ~ the mirror. Therefore, recognition in the mirror is at the same time imaginary misrecognition (méconnaissance) and leads to a subject's split between the imaginary subject 'moi' and the social 'je'. This is the reason for the seemingly paradox sentence 'The I is not the Me', '*Le je n'est pas le moi.*' Important objections have been raised against the importation of Lacanian categories into feminist theory ~ above all by those who resented the fact that Lacan's approach contains and preserves ideas conceptualized by Sigmund Freud. By claiming the subject as the effect of a representative closure, corporeality becomes an outward appearance to which there is no access. Subjectivity thus is locatable in a psychoanalytic interpretation of the repressed, rejected or negated effects of corporeality only. Corporeal feminism ~ a term invented by Elizabeth Grosz ~ has very often engaged in an alliance with psychoanalysis in the past.[44] The Lacanian subject suffers from an incurable defect from the start ~ it lacks. This lack starts with birth because the child is thrown out of the bliss of his embryonic existence. With the separation from its mother's breast, the child experiences the second existential lack, which is reinforced by the alienation in the mirror image. This incompleteness has to be adjusted for provisionally ~ according to Lacan ~ by objects, even though the striving for objects cannot achive the abolition of incompleteness. This is the theoretical foundation of a theory of desire with Lacan.

Without delving too deeply into the history of Lacan's and Freud's concepts within corporeal feminism, it may be important to emphasize the following: Following Freund and Lacan, representation, meaning and subjectivity are located around the notion of lack.[45] Maternal, preoedipal, preconscious fullness is negated in the movement that creates the subject. Identity is the effect of difference that represents the negation of the original identity. For Lacan the subject remains alienated and this alienation is the consequence of the denial of fullness.[46] Feminist theory has appropriated some parts of this theory, especially the metaphor of the castration as negative expression of fullness. Even Judith Butler's discussion of the lesbian phallus

44. Grosz, *Volatile Bodies: Toward a Corporeal Feminism*, vii. Pertaining to the importance of psychoanalysis see Rosi Braidotti, "The Politics of Ontological Difference, " in *Between Feminism and Psychoanalysis*, ed. Teresa Brennan (London, New York: Routledge, 1989), 89-105. Quoted in Bray and Colebrook, "The Haunted Flesh," 47.

45. "L'objet de la psychanalyse n'est pas l'homme; c'est ce qui lui manque, ~ non pas manque absolu, mais manque d'un objet. Encore faut-il s'entendre sur le manque dont il s'agit, c'est celui qui met hors de question qu'on en mentionne l'objet." Jacques Lacan, "Réponses à des étudiants en philosophie sur l'objet de la psychanalyse," in *Les Cahiers pour l'analyse*, publiés par le cercle d'Epistémologie de l'Ecole Normale Supérieure, no. 3 (mai-juin 1966), http://www.lutecium.org/pro.wanadoo.fr/espace.freud/topos/psycha/psysem/lacan66.htm, accessed January 15, 2008.

46. Jacques Lacan, *Ecrits: A Selection* (New York: Norton, 1977), 292-325; Jacques Lacan, *The Four Fundamental Concepts of Psycho-Analysis* (New York: Norton, 1978), 112-118; 244-246; 272-276.

begins with a critical approval of the castration matrix. Prelinguistic fullness is sometimes equated with the principal of the maternal.[47]

Feminist or queer theory that rejects the philosophy of lack has to be able to offer resistance to the territorializing forces of the lack, thereby setting free desire as disconnected from deficiency. Referring to D|G, Guy Hocquenghem wrote in 1972,

> "There is one organ, one sexual organ only, at the center of the Oedipal triangle, the One which determines the place to be occupied by the other three elements of the triangle. The One creates the lack; it determines the absence or presence; the penis envy of the little girl, or the castration fear of the little boy. As the signifying despot, it organizes the global situations of people. As the complete detached object, it plays, in the sexuality of out society, the role money plays in the capitalist economy; the fetish, the veritable universal reference of activity, economic in one case, desiring in the other."[48]

D|G offer such a post-Lacanian theory of desire, in which desire comes in as an autonomous force that not only opposes social determination but constructs the social realm in multiple ways.[49] Gayatri Chakravorty Spivak sympathetically calls Deleuze's concept of desire a 'nominalist catachresis.'[50] Desire for D|G is a real, material, productive and overfilling force. It is dislodged from need. Needs are nothing but the effects of desire, thus making desire a self-propelling social energy.[51] It is important to note that the Deleuzian *désir* must not be confounded with needs, lust or lack.[52] Because it is not internal to the subject,

---

47. Bray and Colebrook, "The Haunted Flesh," 54.

48. "Il y a un organe, un organe sexuel seulement, qui est au centre de la triangulation oedipienne, le Un qui donne leur place aux trois élément du triangle. C'est lui qui construit le manque, c'est lui le signifiant despotique par rapport auquel se créent des personnes globales. Il est l'objet complet détaché qui joue dans la sexualité de notre société le rôle de l'argent dans l'économie capitaliste: le fétiche, la véritable référence universelle de l'activité, économique dans un cas, désirante dans l'autre." Guy Hocquenghem, *Le désir homosexuel* (Paris: Fayard, 2000), 94 f. See Guy Hocquenghem, "Family, Capital, Anus," URL http://www.semiotexte.com/documentPage/familyCapitalAnus.html, accessed 26 June 2009.

49. Stevie Schmiedel, "With or Without Lacan? Becoming-Woman between the Language of Organs and the Anorganism of Language," in *theory@buffalo* 8, http://wings.buffalo.edu/theory/archive/archive.html, accessed January 19, 2008.

50. Gayatri Chakravorty Spivak, *A Critique of Postcolonial Reason: Toward a History of the Vanishing Present* (Cambridge, MA: Harvard University Press, 1999), 251.

51. Teresa Ebert, "For a Red Pedagogy: Feminism, Desire, and Need," *College English*, vol. 58, no. 7 (1996): 795-819, 797.

52. Alice Jardine, "Women in Limbo: Deleuze and His Brothers," *SubStance*, vol. 13, no. 3-4, issues 44-45 (1984): 46-60, 48.

desire cannot be related to lack.[53] "[...D]esire is understood by Deleuze [...] as immanent, as positive and productive, a fundamental, full and creative relation. [...] desire is what produces the real."[54] With the refutation of lack comes the dismissal of the phallus's centrality and the Oedipus complex. Guy Hocquenghem has called this movement 'la protestation contre le découpage oedipien' or the protest against oedipal carving up.[55]

> "Castration is at once the common lot ~ that is, the prevalent and transcendent Phallus, and the exclusive distribution that presents itself in girls as desire for the penis, and in boys as fear of losing it or refusal of a passive attitude. This something in common must lay the foundation for the exclusive use of the disjunctions of the unconscious ~ and teach us resignation [...] ~ in short, 'assumption of one's sex.'"[56]

'Women' and 'Men' according D|G are not subjects that lack, that suffer from penis envy or fear of castration, but machinic *agencements*, desiring machines or bodies without organs, configurations of the masculine and the feminine which communicate with each other constantly without having something in common.[57] Instead of fixed sexes, according to D|G, there is a microscopic transsexuality that is produced by women incorporating integrating men and vice versa.[58] This position dissolves gender duality on a molecular level.

Becoming Gay ~ a stage in becoming-minoritarian?

Homosexuality is positioned centrally by both D|G and Deleuze as a single author. There are several more than passing remarks in Deleuze's books on Sacher-Masoch and on Marcel Proust. In *Proust et les signes* Deleuze dedicated several pages to Proust's homosexuality in order to underline his opposition to the run-of-the-mill interpretation of Proust's homosexuality as inversion.[59] Even if there is not one authorative text by Deleuze on

---

53. Gilles Deleuze and Claire Parnet, *Dialogues* (Paris: Champs, 1977), 108.

54. Elizabeth Grosz, "A Thousand Tiny Sexes: Feminism and Rhizomatics," in *Deleuze and Guattari: Critical As-sessments of Leading Philosophers*, ed. Gary Genosko (London, New York: Routledge, 2001), 1440-1463, 1448.

55. Guy Hocquenghem, *Le désir homosexuel*, 162.

56. Deleuze and Guattari, *Anti-Oedipus*, 67.

57. " [...] neither is there anything in common between the two sexes, nor do they cease communicating with each other [...]" Deleuze and Guattari, *Anti-Oedipus*, 67.

58. Deleuze and Guattari, *Anti-Oedipus*, 325; Jardine, "Women in Limbo," 50.

59. Didier Eribon, "Gilles Deleuze," in *Dictionnaire des cultures gays et lesbiennes* (Paris: Larousse, 2003).

homosexuality, Deleuze has taken up a queer position in his practice of writing and his intimate cooperation with Felix Guattari and Claire Parnet.[60]

"Nous sommes hétérosexuels statistiquement ou molairement, mais homosexuels personnellement, sans le savoir ou en le sachant, et enfin trans-sexués élémentairement, moléculairement."[61] "We are statistical and molar heterosexuals, but personal homosexuals, without knowing it, and finally elementary and molecular transsexuals." Molarly, a human being may be a man or a woman, heterosexual or homosexual, but on a molecular level, this human entity is always polymorphously perverse, because its desire does not have a target. It goes without saying that Deleuze does not consider the term perverse a negative one. D|G perceive the homosexual as a minoritarian stage, but both authors fail to include homosexuality in their writing about becoming. D|G mention homosexuality in *A Thousand Plateaus* passingly and in a treacherous context that borders on homophobia. Speaking about imitation in the context of becoming-woman, the authors assert, "We are not, however, overlooking the importance of imitation, or moments of imitation, among certain homosexual males, muss less the prodigious attempt at a real transformation on the part of certain transvestites."[62] This is where I see a problem: Deleuze's works have been used over and over again by others who worked in the context of *Queer Theory*. (Grosz, 1995; Edelman, 1995; Giffney, 2004); a special edition of *Rhizomes* even suggests that in consonance with Deleuze a new form of *queerness* can be defined. On the other hand, Deleuze refused to be identified as queer himself. This has been criticized by activists and theoreticians of *Queer*. Jeffrey Cohen and Todd Ramlow remarked recently:

> "The evidence for the queerness of Gilles Deleuze is scant. He collaborated passionately with Félix Guattari, radical psychoanalyst and activist for the rights of gays and lesbians. He shared his work and interpenetrated ideas with Michel Foucault, the founding figure of contemporary queer theory. Yet the philosopher spent his life happily married to his wife, Fanny. They raised two children in what looks to us like the predictable structure of a bourgeois family. He was not even an especially spiffy dresser."[63]

60. Kitty Millet, "A Thousand Queer Plateaus: Deleuze's 'Imperceptibility' as a Liberated Mapping of Desire," in *Rhizomes* 11, fall 2005, http://www.rhizomes.net/issue11/millet.html, accessed January 15, 2008.

61. "We are heterosexual statistically or in a molar sense, but homosexual personally, whether we know it or not, and finally transexual [sic] in an elementary or molecular sense", Deleuze and Guattari, *L'Anti-Oedipe, Capita-lisme et schizophrenie* (Paris, 1972), cited in Hocquenghem, *Le désir homosexuel*, 182.

62. Deleuze and Guattari, *A Thousand Plateaus*, 304.

63. Jeffrey J. Cohen and Todd R. Ramlow, "Pink Vectors of Deleuze: Queer Theory and

Michel Cressole, gay activist, author of *Une folle à sa fenêtre* and one of the first scholars to publish a biographical essay on Deleuze in 1973, took a very critical stance on whether Deleuze's work was adaptable to queer studies, especially given Deleuze's own sexuality. Cressole attacked Deleuze for profiting from the experiments of others, homosexuals, drug addicts, alcoholics, masochists and insane people.[64] With homosexuals on the top of his list of Deleuzian victims, he branded Deleuze as a theoretical parasite, who expropriated groups that led an already precarious existence. Cressole assaulted Deleuze, because he had refused to mark himself as consumer of other people's social transgressions or as transgressor himself.[65] Deleuze countered with a remarkable letter that was published under the title 'I have nothing to admit' and that even found its way into Cressole's book on Deleuze in a somewhat altered form.[66] Deleuze addressed the real problem: It was not about the acceptance of a gay identity, it was about the deterritorialization of the subject through the multiplicity of molecular sexes. What was there to know about Deleuze, since he believed in secrets and the power of deception, but not in representation? If he preferred to lead a stationary life, if he did not travel, then because he was on an internal voyage. According to Deleuze, the interesting question was not whether he profited from somebody else, but what people were doing on the corners and how all this was interrelated. "We have to counter people who think 'I'm this, I'm that,' and who do so, moreover, in *psychoanalytic terms* (relating everything to their childhood or fate), by thinking in strange, fluid, unusual terms: I don't know what I am ~ I'd have to investigate and experiment with so many things in a non-narcissistic, non-oedipal way ~ no gay can ever definitively say 'I'm gay.' It's not a question of being this or that sort of human, but of becoming inhuman, of a universal animal becoming ~ not seeing yourself as some dumb animal, but unraveling your body's human organization, exploring this or that zone of bodily intensity, with everyone discovering their own particular zones, and the groups, populations, species that inhabit them."[67]

Confessing to be homosexual, bisexual, gay or queer was in direct contradiction to Deleuze's understanding of practical philosophy, which aimed at becoming minoritarian. The obviously treacherous silence, the empty link

Inhumanism," in *Rhizomes* 11/12 fall 2005/spring 2006, http://www.rhizomes.net/issue11/cohenramlow.html, accessed January 20, 2008.

64. Michel Cressole, *Deleuze* (Paris: Éditions Universitaires, 1973), 112.

65. Kitty Millet, "A Thousand Queer Plateaus".

66. Gilles Deleuze, "Cher Michel, je na'i rien a avouer," in *La Quinzaine litteraire*, 116 (April 1-15, 1973): 17-19.

67. Gilles Deleuze, *Negotiations*: 1972-1990 (New York: Columbia University Press), 11. Also printed as Gilles Deleuze, "Letter to a Harsh Critic" http://www.generation-online.org/p/fpdeleuze4.htm, accessed January 20, 2008.

"becoming-gay" in the branched-out chain of becomings, i.e. 'becoming-woman, becoming-child, becoming-animal, etc.' cannot be arranged within the chain, because it would have represented a visibility that D|G would have rejected.

Nevertheless, becoming-gay could have a place in D|G and in queer theory: It opens a line of flight from heteronormativity that does not necessarily lead to a coming out but that releases practices that are arranged crosswise to the chain of signifiers 'woman, child, animal, plant, mineral', thus making possible a corporeal practice that embodies the dissolution of a majoritarian corporeal practice, thus leaving the logic of oedipal subjectivation. As a consequence, however, becoming-woman would lose its privileged position as a starting point of becomings, thus reducing the inherent stereotypization of woman in Deleuzian philosophy.

Norbert Finzsch

All About My Mother's Shame

Abstract: This paper recounts a joyful day that gives way to the quiet hostility of family relations. In turn this prompts an act of reclamation that gives voice to two men whose stories would otherwise be lost in familial shame. In trying to understand what we experience as shame the paper explores shame by drawing on Lynne Huffer's exploration of Foucault's use of the term bourgeois as correlative with Nietzsche's 'rise of the sovereign moral subject'. This leads to Didier Eribon's reflection on the social power of 'insult' through which shame becomes an enduring process, the condition of the stigmatised subject.

Hopefully what is written here will be understood in the spirit of what is intended: a reflection on a happy day and an unhappy response. It is clearly autobiographical, a sort of boys own story, a reminiscence that is also a 'sort of' essay that is in turn a curious leap into language. Indeed a mixed response to some disturbingly strong emotions: my anger, my partner William's disbelief and my mother's shame.

Making a Decision

We, my partner and I, had discussed the idea of civil partnership for a number of years with varying degrees of enthusiasm, politically opposed to anything that might forge what we perceive to be a normalisation of 'relations' such a formal recognition might afford to us (old lefties that we are) and simultaneously thinking about each other should either of us meet with our demise. Our concern was most certainly for the welfare of the other person and the fact that we know only too well how badly families can behave circling like wolves, when there is the possibility of financial gain. Eventually two incidents forced us to the edge: firstly William's nephew Ian (also gay) died of leukaemia and much to our horror his longstanding partner of 10 years, Mark, was quickly marginalised by the rest of that particular family. He was excluded from being party to the settling Ian's estate. Secondly William had a health scare and in view of his brother's behaviour over his son, Ian's death we made the decision to formalise our own longstanding, to use a very 1970s phrase, 'affair'. We busied ourselves with imagining the when and the where of this event. Clearly for us it had to take place in Edinburgh, our shared 'almost' place of origin. We had no desire to engage in the often reported comedic campery that occasionally belies such public declarations. No performance, no palaver. No oaths, no pledges of allegiance or declarations of monogamy. We know each other way to well for that. No leather enhancing bodily forms of erotic posture or the revelatory fluidity of rubber ~ enhancing every crease of bound flesh, for these are bodies carefully crafted through the judicious intake of alcohol and good food ~ no, none of that. Once the official papers were inscribed it was to be a quiet, elegant affair at one of Edinburgh's finest

urt
nger
itterness
ove

restaurants, the Witchery. We decided only to invite our immediate 'queer family' those proxy siblings with whom we share our lives, for neither of us is particularly close to those who's familial claim is based on blood. Both William's brother and my mother believe that 'blood is thicker than water' regardless of the fact that little effort has been made on their part over the years to foster any meaningful relations with us or to deepen such family ties. For them what this idea 'family' really means is that they have a right of inheritance regardless of their emotional distance, their lack of effort, their absence from our existence. And while I might want to invoke that old cliché and protest that blood is most certainly *not* thicker than water I will refrain from doing so in the usual way, for while this familiar queer cultural reiteration is an attempt to imagine other ways of defining who and what we are, blood *is* actually thicker than water for where water may quench our thirst, while it may soak us, dry and leave little or no trace, blood is materially viscous and sticky, it marks us and leaves an indelible stain that is harder to remove from our skin, from our hands and from our selves.

Yet Another [Not] Coming Out Story

The blood of this story moves on two continents: Europe and North America. It involves the lives of two great-uncles: Peter Morison and Alexander Hamilton, one from either side of my family. I name them fully here as a recuperative act of remembrance for they deserve to be remembered. Peter lived in the small village I grew up in while Alexander, having left Scotland as a child in the 1930s, lived his life in New York. I recount this because in a strange way both of them were somehow central to the families around them and yet not so. Both were simultaneously seen and unseen, hiding in plain view, which in an odd way makes me think of the story of Herculine Barbin[1], quite different I know, as described in Oscar Panizza's novella, *A Scandal in the Convent.* As recounted by Foucault Panizza's main protagonist, Alexina, is described as inhabiting a 'vast area of shadow' at the centre of that particular story. This recollection has some purchase here for both Peter and Alexander could be understood as occupying the space of the family in a similar way, as being present to others if not wholly acknowledged by them. My own knowledge of them is fragmented. I know more about Peter than I do about Alexander simply because of our proximity in space and time, the social space of the village, the private space of the home and the time of my growing up. Alexander I only ever encountered when on his visits to Scotland in the 1970s and 80s when he would arrive

1. M. Foucault, *Herculine Barbin: Being the Recently Discovered Memoirs of a 19th Century French Hermaphrodite* (New York: Pantheon Books, 1980), xvi.

on the QE2. It all seemed very glamorous to me, a working class boy, for he spoke with a strangely unfamiliar accent: Scottish-American I guess and as my olfactory memory permits me to recall, I think, he smoked strangely sweet cigarettes. He always travelled with his sister.

I guess what is already written here hints at their comparable homosexuality if we make assumptions about 'vast areas of shadow' and travelling with sisters, but their homosexuality, which now seems to have been an *open secret* was never spoken about or alluded to in either family except in moments of oblique gossiping in which nothing in particular is addressed in order to maintain the denial of any such possibility of being. Peter's 'true love', we were assured, 'well apparently she died in the war [WWII]' a comment that was very effective in halting any enquirer in their tracks, 'Oh', they would say. So no one would dare to ask Peter directly because the family's assumed position on the subject, the narrative told, was that it was too painful for him to speak. It was best left alone. This was not borne out of a family's decision to deliberately close ranks to protect the family's reputation but rather it seemed to be something that was handed down generationally, something that was much more organic in form, something that coalesced over time.

As I grew up I became attuned to Peter's existence, to the stories of his youth in which as he said, 'he took to 'tap''.[2] I also became aware of the things he would say that didn't quite make sense ~ or made another sense ~ and to the cryptic comments offered up in the silence that defined the family's dinner times. I have a bricolage of memories that seem to add up to something that, of course, has never been verified by the two men I am speaking about but as I grew up I seemed to learn how to know. I 'recognised' them. For some reason I knew that I 'knew' them, well at least one of them, somehow. There are many moments that create these portraits, too many to mention here but there are two which seem to me to be significant: firstly when I first visited New York, 5 years after Alexander's death, the family insisted on informing me of their progress from their point of arrival in the US in the 1930s until the then present day [1990]. We watched film after film on VHS, some of which was fascinating cine footage that had been transferred onto tape. But the moment of significance was that in a film from 1963 or thereabouts, in which Alexander is dancing with a woman, at what seemed to be a wedding or function, one of the assembled party exclaimed, 'Look Alex *did* kiss that woman!' There was a palpable sigh of relief from all in the room, from his 95 year old sister, from his nephews and nieces. It was a very odd moment, this need to re-affirm him

2. One of his most relished stories was of when he decided to become a tap dancer and in order to practice received a tap dancing set, common in the 1950s, which consisted of a pair of tap shoes and a small square sheet of hardboard as an appropriate surface on which to tap.

as a heterosexual man in front of this stranger, this relative who had come to visit from the homeland. Up until that point I hadn't given it much thought, I wasn't particularly looking for evidence but this moment was electrifying. I began to pay attention to every word about him and realised how little I knew. For example, I didn't know he lived in Greenwich Village, nor that he walked rich people's dogs to make a living, nor that he lived in a rather small grim apartment. The more I found out, the stylishly exotic figure *cruising* on the QE2 slowly diminished. His solitary life style hadn't really come to mind but the recounting of his story has left a residual mark.

The second disturbingly telling moment concerns Peter for upon his death in 1992, my mother who had ~ strangely enough ~ been very close to him, phoned to tell me he had died. His estranged brother stepped in as next of kin and took control of what needed to be done. Peter left no will which was actually neither here nor there as there was very little of value to mark this life that was. He was not a materialist person. But she, who had looked after him at the behest of her own mother ~ his sister ~ for over 20 years suddenly found herself unwanted and closed out. She was afforded no respect, the emotional impact of his death on her was not acknowledged and she had no place in this familial reorientation. She phoned me a second time a few days later, to tell me that when she had gone to Peter's home, she had walked in on his brother, Andrew (named here by me in order to shame his shameful behaviour) putting Peter's photographic archive ~ of his life and that of the family ~ into the kitchen sink. He then covered the photographs in bleach. My mother's protests were ignored. They both knew I wanted the archive. She was told that no one would have it. Peter was being erased from the 'family'. This act of erasure was shameful and cruel and not unconnected, I would say, to the shame and the cruelty of the classical canon. Therefore, it is with these words I am trying to give a sense of him, it is with these words I am trying to write him back into existence for as Muriel Spark's character, Jean Brodie might say ~ in a highly affected Morningside accent I might add ~ 'There little girl, you are inscribed!'

The Shame of it All

Shame is a very powerful feeling regardless of the situation and retelling this story reminds me of something Lynne Huffer notes in the *Queer Moralities* chapter of her book, *Mad for Foucault: Rethinking the Foundations of Queer Theory,* in which she addresses Foucault's treatise on madness. In her analysis she reminds us that in *Madness* Foucault repeatedly posits the word *bourgeois* as identifying a historical shift that she regards as corresponding to Nietzsche's 'the rise of the sovereign moral subject'. In doing so she argues that we should consider the conceptualisation of the *bourgeois* in Foucault's work, less in relationship to the work of Reich and Marcuse and the rhetoric of the repressed libido but rather to view it through a 'Nietzschean lens' that allows for a reinterpretation of the term *bourgeois* as marking 'the rise of the private sphere as the privileged site for the production of moral norms.' With this in mind *bourgeois* for Huffer can be understood as meaning 'family' and as such it can be argued that this is linked to what she describes as today's 'ethico-moral policing mechanisms of "family values"', values predicated on scandal, guilt and shame.[3] As Foucault reminds us the production of subjectivity is actually a matter of the 'internalisation of man as shame'. A statement with which Foucault is following the Nietzschean description of bad conscience, the *serious illness* of bad conscience that is a 'rejection of the body through its internalisation as shame' which was understood as a reason*able* bloody and cruel price to be paid for "the whole sombre thing called reflection", for as Huffer recounts Nietzsche is preoccupied with self-repugnance, with the 'swamp of shame' which she characterises as playing out the 'moral consequences of the Cartesian sacrifice of the body for the mind.' The moral subject, as described by Nietzsche, therefore "holds his nose" at his own body.[4]

Here it is also worth recalling that for Sartre shame marks the point at which the subject becomes an object not only to the other but also to itself. Shame is therefore the realisation of a schism, of a fundamental asymmetry in the shaping of any subjectivity and as Didier Eribon succinctly reminds us, 'It all begins with an insult.'[5] Insult has a fundamental relationship to shame and as such a particular impact on the formation of the subject. To be publicly shamed, in the family or social setting, is a traumatic event, an event that lingers in the psyche for the insult is much more than that which it describes, an individual, it is also a judgement: 'a verdict'. Insult is about power, the power that one person has, or wishes to have, over another for as Eribon declares,

> "I discover that I am a person about whom something can be said, to whom something can be said, someone who can be looked at or talked about in a certain way and who is stigmatised by that gaze and those words. The act of naming produces an awareness of oneself as other, transformed by others into an object."[6]

The subject is wounded by words: *faggot, dyke, nigger* and so on, and perhaps more forcefully so when the word *dirty* is used as the prefix. Such insulting

---

3. Lynne Huffer, *Mad for Foucault: Rethinking the Foundations of Queer Theory* (New York: Columbia University Press, 2010), 105-106.
4. Huffer, *Mad for Foucault: Rethinking the Foundations of Queer Theory*, 105-106.
5. Didier Eribon, *Insult and the Making of the Gay Self* (London: Duke University Press, 2004), 15.
6. Eribon, *Insult and the Making of the Gay Self*, 16.

remarks tell the subject that the perpetrator has the power to hurt them but not only that to indelibly mark them with hurt. The hurt subject is diminished, controlled, contained, reduced and reminded of his or her position as 'not like others, not normal', or to instantiate a more poetic gesture from Jean Genet's *La Galerie*, 'a dizzying word, arriving from the foundations of the world, destroyed its happy order'.[7] What is set in motion here is the enactment of performative utterances that Eribon, while drawing on the work of J. L. Austin, identifies as injurious speech acts whose 'function is to produce certain effects ~ notably, to establish or to renew the barrier between "normal" people and those [Erving] Goffman calls "stigmatised" people and to cause the internalisation of that barrier within the individual being insulted.' As Eribon observes, 'Insult tells me what I am to the extent that it makes me be what I am.'[8]

I cast my mind back to the *open secret* for rather than being a structure that protects ~ indeed whom does it protects? ~ it is also really a form of insult for the maintenance of silence, the acknowledged lack of acknowledgement, the knowing without saying is also an attempt to control, to have power over the subject and the situation. In one sense this is actually more insidious for it is perpetrated by those who are often closest to the individual concerned, those who have a vested interest in that person and in some respect those who perhaps perceive themselves as having more to lose within the wider society: those who constitute the 'family'. However, insult as shame, or rather insult as the mechanism by which the internalisation of shame marks the condition of the subject's formation, is also about fear and rarely simply fear about the difference of another but rather that of the perpetrating moral subject's own sense of instability. As Huffer points out the moral subject learns to reject the hideous stink and filth of the body in order to maintain its own 'reasoned' sense of coherence.

The Dutiful Love of a Parent

When I undertook my own rite of passage, when my own story unfolded, my mother was the one who responded badly. To her it was she who, as a parent, had done something wrong. It was her who had nurtured her children badly. Of course she already knew, she must have known for my childhood was defined by adult conversations that I sometimes seemed to be 'just like Uncle Peter'. No one ever really explained what this meant at the time, and I never

---

7. Jean Genet, "La Galerie" in his *Poemes*, 51 as quoted in Eribon, *Insult and the Making of the Gay Self*, 356.

8. Eribon, *Insult and the Making of the Gay Self*, 17.

asked what made me like him, but then I didn't really have to. I now know that my mother didn't want to know what she knew she didn't want it to be true, this thing that was defined by an absence of speech. She didn't want to believe it and if it remained unsaid it could *never* be true. But it was said and it is true. In 1987 I moved to London, I came out, I became militant. I was angry, I protested against the insidious Clause 28 and the wider injustices of a 'democratic' system that does not afford respect to all of its citizens. But the distance I had travelled was not enough. The journey was incomplete. I could speak publicly to close friends but not to my parents, and certainly not to my mother. I calculated her response, I told myself it would be fine, after all she was my mother and she loves me. I called to say I had something to say and that I would visit them. She said 'ok'. I travelled 462 miles. When I arrived they were waiting, watching television in front of an open coal fire. I sat in front of them. I looked at them, they looked at me. My father urged me to 'spit it out'. I said what I had to say. My father raised his newspaper, grunted and said no more. My mother cried. I returned to London.

Over the next year or so I maintained periodic contact as my mother decided that she loved me but did not like me, in that she did not like what I was but loved me because as she said, 'you are my son', a statement of fact but also words that described a burden that she bears. I told her that to me the love she spoke of was a duty love, a matter of blood, an obligation. It was not the unconditional love that a parent has for a child. There was no response. Of course what was at stake here was not the experience of a child as an adult, coming to terms with their own sense of self, but rather my declaration was something that she had decided was happening to her, something that, if people knew, would diminish her status as a person in the community she is part of. She feared being ostracised which is understandable, but as good Scottish Calvinists and Catholics do, she wore her shame well.

Over time we seemed to be able to speak to each other on the phone, or at the very least we seemed to be able to be civil and upon meeting William, and because he was based in Edinburgh, she seemed to accept us as we are. In a way as our relationship developed, she (indeed they) seemed to delight in our visits and in our weekend forays into parts of Scotland and Northumbria neither had never taken the time to visit. I was being, indeed we were being, the dutiful sons. But upon the registering of our civil partnership and upon revealing this to my immediate family my mother's response was chilling and the word 'congratulations' was a word she could not utter, a word she did not understand. After my sister's intervention my mother called again. She was conciliatory but her voice was trembling. Eventually it became apparent that she was fearful that others in the village of my birth would 'find out' on social media, on Facebook, which she imagines to be beyond her control. In the end, while angered by her response and yet in recognising her fear, I promised we wouldn't 'advertise' our happy day with our 'other family' of stigmatised friends. What is interesting here is not that my mother is ashamed but rather that she too has become a stigmatised subject, for the parent of a gay, lesbian or trans child often imagines her or himself to be relocated in the social structure, for society, or at least the society of such small and closely knit and vaguely religious communities will undoubtedly attribute blame. Her fear is primarily a fear of being cast as a 'bad mother', as having allowed something to go wrong, or of not recognising that something had indeed gone very wrong. But this is not simply a matter of external pressure for what this story tells us is that she has *always already* accepted responsibility, she has responded to her sense of shame as a burden she must carry, as she now often tells us 'to her grave', which is also a process of internalisation. *My mother is a woman with melodramatic tendencies.* What is significant is that her shame simultaneously prefigures and is prefigured by my shame, the shame she, as a moral subject who is filled with shame, believes I should feel above and beyond the shame that she is responding to: a shame that we might define as mine, the primary shameful experience voiced. However, this dual and perhaps dynamic sense of shame that has defined our relationship demands its renegotiation for only then can we move beyond the physiological prefigured effects of 'our shame' that enables both subjects, moral and stigmatised, to effect change. What has become apparent is that this shame, our shame, is not necessarily something that we can 'get over' for it is the foundation of what we are, and in that respect it is similar to 'coming out' in that it is not a single traumatic event, it is, as is the subject of insults, an enduring process.

The idea that shame is always somehow prefigured reminds us that 'the world of insults pre-exist the birth of the stigmatised subject' and if we recall Judith Butler's discussion of hate speech it is less a question of the stigmatised subject as the object of someone else's hateful speech but rather that it is a matter of recognition, 'one does not exist because one is "recognised" but because one is "recognisable".'[9] And this is for Butler ~ with regard to language ~ as it was for Louis Althusser before her ~ with regard to ideology ~ a matter of 'interpellation'.[10] Here the 'subject' is simultaneously recognised as the

---

9. Judith Butler, *Excitable Speech: A Politics of the Performative* (New York: Routledge, 1997), 5-6.

10. Eribon, *Insult and the Making of the Gay Self*, 56. The following is paraphrased from Eribon's commentary, 'For Althusser "ideology interpellates individuals as subjects" which he explains through what he calls a "little theoretical theatre" in which he imagines a police agent yell at someone: "Hey, you there!" Althusser goes on to say, "Assuming that the theoretical scene I have imagined takes place in the street, the hailed individual will turn round. By this mere one-hundred-and eighty-degree physical conversion, he becomes a subject. Why? Because he has recognised that the hail was 'really' addressed to him, and that 'it was really him who was hailed' (and not someone else)." What Althusser is getting at here is that 'in the real functioning of ideology' it is clear that "the existence of ideology and the hailing or interpellation of individuals as subjects are one and the same thing" and what he gives us

'subjected', in that the subject is always already subjected to that which it is born into that which lies in wait ~ 'the subjectivity and the social imprint are one and the same: the individual "subject" is produced by interpellation, that is to say, by cognitive (and therefore social) structures' ~ and as Eribon goes on to remind us, 'insult is one of the most remarkable (or most concrete) forms of what Althusser has (abstractly and metaphorically) designated as interpellation.'[11] But does this really mean, as Sartre suggests in speaking of the young Gustave Flaubert that 'processes lie in wait' for us 'as do the role to be played'?[12] Is the world "insulting" as Eribon claims, 'because it is structured according to hierarchies that carry with them the possibility of insult'? While these questions are rhetorical it is clear that the interruption, the interpellation in the normalised structure demands more for when I think of my mother and me we are both marked by language and the emotional impact of words in many different and often contradictory ways. Insult, shame, anger, bitterness and love are therefore bound together as the condition of the interpellated stigmatised subject. Sometimes it is difficult to understand how love can accommodate shame, bitterness and anger but can I assure you dear friends it does.

is an understanding that the subject is always already born into that which always already is: a world shaped by ideology.'

11. Eribon, *Insult and the Making of the Gay Self*, 57.

12. Eribon, *Insult and the Making of the Gay Self*, 61.

Stephen Kennedy

Echostate

Abstract: Echostate is the result of a paper given as part of the Oscillation Series (http://sonictheory.com/?p=427) organised by the Sonic Theory group at Humboldt University in Berlin and moderated by Jan Thoben and Shintaro Miyazake. The presentation was in the form of a virtual interactive performance that also included an original score (http://vimeo.com/24087954). The piece follows the anti-ocular logic of Jean Luc Nancy and coins a new term Echostate that is intended to offer an alternative to static representational thinking. The main aim is to argue that the formation of materiality in digital environment is a sonic rather than a visual phenomenon.

Echostate is a term related to Michel Foucault's category 'statement', in combination with Gaston Bachelard's use of 'reverberation' and 'echo' in his introduction to The Poetics of Space. The term expands the scope of the original concepts by examining how statements are echoed and amplified across a range of media that now exist in multiple simultaneous forms ~ repeatable but not always identical in as much as they can take on numerous different digitally enabled forms.

Statements are more than abstract signs, they are operational performances that cohere with objects to create a kind of materiality that is repeatable and, melodic rhythmic and harmonious. They are not to be cited themselves as examples for fear of rendering them static, and creating empty signifiers. Instead they must be recognised as modulating incessantly in a dispersed fashion that makes them difficult to tie down and to have representational meaning assigned to them. This is why they are so significant and powerful. They very definitely exist but not always in the way that we expect them to.

> "We will call statement the modality of existence proper to that group of signs: a modality that allows it to be something more than a series of traces, something more than a succession of marks on a substance, something more than a mere object made by a human being; a modality that allows it to be in relation with a domain of objects, to prescribe a definite position to any possible subject, to be situated among other verbal performances, and to be endowed with a repeatable materiality."[1]

1. Michel Foucault, *The Archaeology of Knowledge* (New York: Vintage Book, 1982), 120.

nti-ocular logic
nteractive
onic materialities
onic theory
chostate

It is the being 'in relation with' that is important here. Statements move through objective space forming bonds with other statements to create conditions of possibility or frameworks, a kind of coherent space within which individuals become accustomed or attuned as to how to operate. He goes on to say that:

> "the term discourse can be defined as the group of statements that belong to a single system of formation..."[2]

These systems of formation, despite appearing stable in so far as they represent a common sense reality, are in a perpetual state of uncertainty. Both statements and discourses move and return as echoes ~ sometimes clear and intact, recognizable and coherent, but always possessing the possibility that they will come back altered or rearranged, or less recognizable, allowing a new or different common sense to prevail.

In so far as the coherence of statements operate to form discourses and conditions of possibility, they are witnessed as echoes identifiable in what Nigel Thrift calls 'practice' which as the third tenet of non representational theory serves to sustain a veneer of stability whilst simultaneously serving as a means of identifying the changing state of things.

Practices like discourses can be identified and analysed in order to make sense of the moment that we find ourselves in and to assess how it differs from previous moments as well as moments to come. Thrift describes this saying:

> "...material bodies are continually being rewritten as unusual circumstances arise, and new bodies are continually making an entrance but, if we are looking for something that approximates to a stable feature of a world that is continually in meltdown, that is continually bringing forth new hybrids, then I take the practice to be it. Practices are productive concatenations that have been constructed out of all manner of resources and which provide the basic intelligibility of the world: they are not therefore the properties of actors but of the practices themselves. Actions presuppose practices and not vice versa...as practices lose their place in a historical form of life, they may leave abandoned wreckage behind them which can then take on new life, generating new hybrids or simply leavings which still have resonance."[3]

2. Foucault, *The Archaeology of Knowledge*, 121.
3. Nigel Thrift, *Non-Representational Theory: Space, Politics, Affect*, (London: Routledge, 2007), 8-9.

Resonant 'leavings' or echoes work as acoustic refrains with disparate and uncertain forms coalescing to create discourses that once identified can melt into air, undergoing a quantum leap before reforming in a newer, or indeed an older, space and time (or spacetime). To understand such complex patterning and re-patterning requires a methodology that does not rely solely on visual stimuli. According to such an approach,[4] specific discursive phenomenon traverse what might be called 'mediated environments', where objects as things, words, concepts, percepts, or Bachelard's poetic images operate in what McLuhan has called an anti-environment that uncouples the figure / ground relationship to focus on the ground alone. This ground is not present on the visual register.[5] It can be described as having the characteristics of a statement without operating as an exemplar or as fixed representation.[6]

Practices become manifest at the point at which statements cohere and begin to reverberate and echo with the 'repeatable materiality' that Foucault identified, only now in a range of guises or forms that may not always be clearly visible. Like Bachelard's poetic image they are formations that are not determined in any causal linear sense by the arrangements that precede them (Minkowski's well spring in Bachelard).[7] Not objects, not substitutes for objects, but resonances that are to be understood on their own terms as real and material but with an as yet uncertain form.

> "The poetic image is not subject to an inner thrust. It is not an echo of the past. On the contrary: through the brilliance of an image, the distant past resounds with echoes, and it is hard to know at what depth these echoes will reverberate and die away."[8]

Bachalard makes the dialectical distinction between soul and mind with the poetic image residing in the former before it is formalized as representation in the latter. "Forces are manifested [He says] in poems that do not pass through

---

4. Sonic Economy: http://www.ctheory.net/articles.aspx?id=649

5. Marshall McLuhan and Eric McLuhan, *Laws of Media: The New Science*, (Toronto: University of Toronto Press, 1992), 3.

6. Foucault's refusal to be drawn into providing examples was an important stance that highlighted the fluid nature of his method that must always be in process and not static in terms of citing fixed examples against which all other cases might be judged. Such a generic taxonomy of statements would be so busy allotting phenomena to their rightful place that it would miss the formation of new discourses as statements moved out of view or as they morphed within and between strict categories.

7. Bachelard, *The Poetics of Space* (Boston, Beacon, 1994), XVI.

8. Bachelard, *The Poetics of Space*, XVI.

the circuits of knowledge".[9] So artists and poets as well as those who engage with their work dwell in the nonrepresentational realm of the soul where affect reigns. The dichotomy of mind and soul like McLuhan's environment / anti environment seems problematic in so far as the artist is situated outside of the so-called real world. In contrast to this the argument is made here that the usefulness of such pursuits is to open up, as Foucault has done, avenues of exploration into social and political formations that are themselves not indifferent or immune to artistic expression.

So established circuits of knowledge in relation to art and other supposedly less creative practices only tell part of any story. But the point is not to separate them off from one another but to recognize the constant interplay between them.

The formation of a discourse, like the poetic image, is equally not caused by or linked to the past in a linear fashion but is rather a process that might appropriate elements of the past ~ re animating them or amplifying an echo that had been dying away or that had been silenced in an archive. Identifying such formations is what Foucault does and it is a process that can be further attuned by the introduction of the sonic so that the dispersed invisibility of arrangements, their stealth, does not render them inaccessible and therefore beyond critique. When obscured by shadows statements may still be heard. This is why a critical understanding of what is happening in terms of music ~ past, present and future ~ should be taken to be a serious political endeavour. Adorno knew this, and Attali still does, but they both have clung to a dialectical approach to some degree. To counter this we should recognise statements as having an amplitude that is significant enough to mark them as recognizable practices whilst also acknowledging that they can dissipate and fragment at any time, or when the 'moment' is right.[10]

So the problem seems to be with representation. Beginning with the question of representation as a field of philosophical inquiry that impacts directly on the ways in which contemporary mediated environments are understood, sonority is presented here as non-representational and as embodying movement.[11] This idea is pivotal if we are to progress beyond what Heidegger calls the ontic, to the ontological as a process that is always in motion and is capable of accounting for the fluid complexities of the contemporary age.[12] To do so is to engage with some fundamental

9. Bachelard, *The Poetics of Space*, XXI.

10. Stuart Elden, "Rhythmanalysis: An Introduction," in Henry Lefebvre, *Rhythmanalysis: Space, Time and Everyday Life*, trans Stuart Elden and Gerald Moore, (London: Continuum, 2004), x.

11. For a longer discussion on movement as a leitmotif of non-representational theory, please see: Thrift, *Non-Representational Theory*, 5ff.

12. The digital information age is itself a discourse formed of statements born of Western scientific rationalism with echoes of classical liberalism and the hippy ideals of the 1960's. It is emitted and returned as it spreads. As we watch the second world industrialize in our own 'image' however,

philosophical questions that go back to classical Greek philosophy and its emphasis on visuality.[13]

In Plato's simile of the cave the light of the sun is proposed as a threshold beyond which the knowing subject cannot progress. Levels of reality are unfolded in a manner that suggests only a theoretical conception of Being. All that can be known is quantitatively present and visible. That which cannot be seen can never be known in any meaningful sense. It was a bias that was reinforced by Aristotle;

> "Above all we value sight because sight is the principle source of knowledge..."[14]

This privileging of the visual realm produces a particular kind of knowledge; a representational kind that names and fixes and renders concepts and phenomena stationary. And it is a system of thought that works, it is reliable and we have grown accustomed to it. But it is also limited. It leaves out much of the important information or is simply incapable of mediating the intensity of feeling that may be present yet difficult to communicate.

As Marco Polo explains to Kublai Kahn when describing a scene from his travels in Italo Calvino's *Invisible Cities*:

> "I could tell you how many steps make up the streets rising like stairways, and the degree of the arcades' curves, and what kind of zinc scales cover the roofs; but I already know this would be the same as telling you nothing. The City does not consist of this, but of relationships between the measurements of its space and the events of its past..."[15]

To communicate the multiplicity of the lived moment that resounds with echoes may require more than simple representational devices. The space between measurements is not an in between as 'in between point a and b' or 'from a to z'; it is a thoroughfare or a medium that is alive and relational, through which sound vibrates and echoes. It is a space where possibilities

---

we run the risk of missing something. The sound of science has emanated from the west and has resounded in the East before rebounding as an echo of vindication, reflected; self congratulatory and isomorphic.

13. McLuhan & McLuhan, *Laws of Media*, 4.

14. Don Hide. *Listening and Voice: Phenomenologies of Sound*, (New York, SUNY, 2007), 7.

15. Italo Calvino, *Invisible Cities*, (New York: Harcourt, 1978), 9.

abound and where multidimensional elements or statements resound, compiling combining, cohering as practices or discourses. We are aided in the task of understanding this by Heidegger in so far as he offers the possibility of a challenge to the dominance of Platonic logic that came to dominate Western philosophy and science, by proposing a re-focused critique of Being or a 'fundamental ontology'. Such a proposal takes us into the realm of the invisible or the not so visible world of shadows where contemplation rather than a gazing upon, prevail.

Junichiro Tanizaki takes up this point in his essay *In Praise of Shadows* wherein he highlights, in a manner comparable to Heidegger, the Western obsession with light and seeing, (a process of getting nature 'in hand' that Heidegger calls Enframing)[16] that took Eastern science and technology in a direction that was not its own. "Imagine," he asks:

> "If we in the Orient had developed our own science. Suppose for instance that we had developed our own physics and chemistry: would not the techniques and industries based on them have taken a different form, would not our myriads of everyday gadgets, our medicines, the products of our industrial art ~ would they not have suited our national temper better than they do? In fact our conception of physics itself, and even the principles of chemistry, would probably differ from that of Westerners; and the facts we are now taught concerning the nature and function of light, electricity, and atoms might well have presented themselves in different form."[17]

Even fundamental scientific principles then are subject to the fluid interplay of statements within discourses, to the arbitrary formation and amplification of ways of thinking that are heard above all others and seen in practices that come to dominate at the expense of dissonant expressions struggling to establish themselves as statements.

The emphasis on light and vision and observation impacts on all aspects of scientific, artistic and cultural life and has even imposed itself as statement, or an echo of a statement (echostate) where contrary conditions of possibility existed but failed to take or keep hold.

Tanizaki goes on to say:

---

16. Martin Heidegger, "The Question Concerning Technology", in *The Question Concerning Technology and Other Essays*, trans W. Lovitt (New York: Harper & Row, 1977).

17. Junichiro Tanizaki, *In Praise of Shadows* (Frankfurt: Springer-Verlag, 1933 / 2010), 14.

> "It has been said of Japanese food that it is a cuisine to be looked at. I would go further and say that it is to be meditated upon, a kind of silent music evoked by the combination of lacquerware and the light of the candle flickering in the dark."[18]

There is much to be gained from entering this shadowy realm, and listening to the silent music of contemplation. If embraced it can prompt a revealing.

As Heidegger says in his essay *The Question Concerning Technology*:

> "Always the unconcealment of that which is goes upon a way of revealing. Always the destining of revealing holds complete sway over man. But that destining is never a fate that compels. For man becomes truly free only insofar as he belongs to the realm of destining and so becomes one who listens and hears, and not one who is simply constrained to obey."[19]

The realm of visual representation and its limited dimensionality then is a philosophical conundrum to which we must return again and again. We might do so by returning not only to Heidegger but also to Schopenhauer and his distinction between representation and the will and to Nietzsche and his Apollonian and Dionysian duality where respectively sonority/music is a copy of the will and an intoxicating force that does not reveal itself on a visual plane. Music for both Schopenhauer and Nietzsche operates on an existential plane or in a parallel world where different rules apply and where alternative realities lie.

Hence if we are to fully understand the nature of our being and by necessity our current plight we need to move out of what Marshall McLuhan called 180 degree visual space and into the 360 degree acoustic/sonic post Euclidian realm.

Drawing on the acoustic/sonic serves to support Foucault in terms of identifying links within a dispersed system of power that relies on its invisibility, its stealth, for its continued success? For Foucault the formation of discourses and their constituent parts are not conveniently and quantifiably visible; they cannot be simply mapped in gridded space that is absolute and static. Rather their movement must be tracked across relative space in all its multidimensional forms.

As Jean Luc Nancy states:

---

18. Tanizaki, *In Praise of Shadows*, 26.
19. Heidegger, "The Question Concerning Technology", 25.

> "There is, at least potentially, more isomorphism between the visual and the conceptual, even if only by virtue of the fact that the morphe, the form implied in the idea of isomorphism is immediately thought or grasped on the visual plane. The sonorous, on the other hand, outweighs form. It does not dissolve it, but rather enlarges it; it gives it an amplitude, a density and a vibration or an undulation whose outline never does anything but approach. The visual persists until its disappearance; the sonorous appears and fades away into its permanence."[20]

Foucault's statements like sound traverse qualitative space ~ fading into permanence to one day be returned as echo. In so being they can be identified along a diagonal vector somewhere between the vertical and horizontal axes of propositions and phrases ~ mobile and atonal.[21]

Unconstrained by the isomorphic extended body, statements come into relation with one another in ways that are not restricted by spatial proximity nor constrained by notions of sensible similarity or difference. In this respect they are qualitative not quantitative.

On this matter Leibniz said in his Metaphysical Foundations of Mathematics:

> "Quantity or magnitude is that in things which can be known only through their simultaneous compresence ~ or by their simultaneous perception... Quality on the other hand, is what can be known in things when they are observed singly, without requiring compresence."[22]

The absence of compresence is equivalent to Foucault's dispersion or Nancy's qualitative 'fading away into permanence'.

Statements move, echo, bounce, collide, connect and disconnect across space and time; not constrained by a knowing subject in Schopenhauer's representational field, not constrained by the body or the soundproof room but released beyond its extension in space ~ escaped from its solidity like the sound from the throat that the speaker does not recognize as their own (Lyotard, 2002). Such formations are acoustic/sonic in ways both literal

---

20. Jean Luc Nancy, *Listening*, trans Charlotte Mandell (New York: Fordham University Press, 2007), 2.

21. Gilles Deleuze, *Negotiations 1972-1990*, trans Martin Joughin (London: Black Dog Press, 1999), 3.

22. Edward S. Casey, *The Fate of Place: A Philosophical History* (Los Angeles: University of California Press, 1998), 171.

and non-literal, dealing specifically with sound but also by using sound as a non-representational model of organization for a multiple range of significant factors.

Such a model could arrange phenomena without fixing them in either space or time ~ allowing them to move in relation to one another, to create narratives without beginning middle or end, to construct archaeologies of the present in the knowledge that at some future point they will need to be constructed anew. The patterns may not be neat, may not follow strict tonal logic, they may not even be patterns that are recognizable in any conventional sense, not ordered according to received notions of difference or similarity, not present in the corridors of power, not attributable to single individuals, not part of a consensual understanding. Yet they are there and they should be understood as being there without having to provide locational evidence. They are capable of evading such techniques and might only be knowable via recourse to, or a drawing upon, the sonic, acoustic, poetic realm of the artist (as creative practitioner in multiple fields) who can create a necessary anti-environment. Yet the idea of the artist itself may need some considerable rethinking.

As phenomena, statements move in relation to one another across three realms of space: Collateral ~ which invokes the relationship between statements in terms of similarity and / or proximity / distance that gets over the problem of compresence in both spatial and temporal terms; Correlative ~ that assess the relationship between statements and their subject; and Associate ~ that assesses the internal institutional logic of statements and the circumstances of their production (Deleuze, The New Archivist).[23] Only by employing each will the complexities of the current age be able to be accounted for. To pursue this task is to respond to Deleuze's comment that:

> "If things aren't going too well in contemporary thought, its because there's a return under the name of 'modernism' to abstractions, back to the problem of origins, all that sort of thing..." [modernism returned as an echo].

He continues:

> "Any analysis in terms of movements, vectors is blocked. We're in a very weak phase, a period of reaction. Yet philosophy thought it had done

23. Heidegger prioritises language in The Question Concerning Technology to the extent that the materiality of the environment in which linguistic practices take place are marginalised. Foucault may also be guilty of this. Deleuze & Guattari reinvigorate the material as words and things interrelate within spatialised realms, mileus or territories where rhythms reconcile the discursive and non-discursive.

> with the problem of origins. It was no longer a question of starting or finishing. The question was rather, what happens in between?"[24]

What happens in these spaces is the mediation of statements, and it is a process that is in constant motion as they correspond with discourses. This involves engaging with sometimes invisible discursive formations or arrangements, statements that are neither compresent or tethered, that operate not in a Platonic transcendent or theoretical realm but in an immanent sensory one. Not only words and things and the causal relationship in either direction, but the intercausal relationship back and forth. Visibilities Deleuze tells us, must be found in things and the way in which we do this is crucial: it is the finding that is important here as a process. For finding implies something is hidden or not immediately present. The manner of a coming into appearance, like the fire that casts the shadow in Plato's cave may not present itself to the observer, thus language and form as medium and or technology ~ or as technologies of power ~ contribute to the way things are lit but they themselves may not always be visible.

We need to find the ways in which statements move and form from the shadowy representations in Plato's Cave to the digital realm. The way this is and has been done can be seen in archives that are themselves audio-visual as language lights up what it is we see and what we see gives rise to language formations in many new forms.[25] Contemporary developments in production storage and distribution of information bring statements into new relations with each other that are not amenable to static representation.

The contemporary lived environment as mediated space invokes dimensionality and a non linear understanding of events that are not simply superseded but remain always as echoes in the audio visual archive ~ sometimes dormant sometimes hyperactive, like musical notes ready to cohere with others in a multiplicity of ways to form scores; not written down but set free. Never stationary but always fluid.[26] Explaining how discourses operate in this way allows us to recognise them not only as regimes of power or as examples of negative dialectics but as sonic components that configure and reconfigure in multidimensional spacetime.

24. Deleuze, *Negotiations 1972-1990*, 121.

25. The description of the archive as audio visual is important here in justifying the wide range of sources / statements that one might draw upon in order to identify a discourse.

26. Gilles Deleuze and Felix Guattari, F. A *Thousand Plateaus: Capitalism and Schizophrenia*, trans Brian Massumi (Minneapolis: University Minnesota Press, 1987), 386.

Hannah Lammin

A Paradoxical Architecture:

Babel, and the Founding of Community Through the Confounding of Tongues

Abstract: Hegel, in his Aesthetics, proposes the Tower of Babel as an architectural symbol that is foundational in the establishment of social unity. This article argues that Babel is a paradoxical symbol for unity, and is emblematic of the difficulty that Hegel's philosophical system presents for understanding community. This problem is shown to be structural, deriving from the essentially architectonic logic of dialectics, and connected to language at a fundamental level. Drawing on the thought of Bataille, Blanchot and Nancy, the spatiality of Hegel's system is turned inside-out, with an "anarchitectural" topology proposed, instead, as the ground of community.

> "In the wide plains of the Euphrates an enormous architectural work was erected; [...] The ensemble of all the peoples at that period worked at this task and since they all came together to complete an immense work like this, the product of their labour was to be a bond which was to link them together by means of the excavated site and ground, the assembled blocks of stone, and the as it were architectural cultivation of the country." ~ G. W. F. Hegel[1]

> "Therefore is the name of it called Babel; because the LORD did there confound the language of all the earth: and from thence did the LORD scatter them abroad upon the face of all the earth." ~ Genesis[2]

Hegel, in his *Aesthetics*, locates the origin of art in symbolic architecture, and the first example he offers of such architecture is the Tower of Babel. He says that the tower, "was built in common, and the aim and content of the work was at the same time the community of those who constructed it."[3] This structure, that according to Hegel functions as a symbol of national unity, forms the foundation of his aesthetics, which describes a dialectical *telos* that moves towards the total conceptual and social unification of Absolute Reason. However, Babel is a strange symbol for teleological unity considering that, according to myth, its construction was never completed, and the project resulted in the confounding of tongues whereby a people who had previously had one language could no longer understand one another, and were scattered across the earth.

1. G. W. F. Hegel, "Architectural Works built for National Unification", *Aesthetics, Lectures on Fine Art*, trans T. M. Knox (Oxford: The Clarendon Press, 1975), 638.
2. Genesis 11:9, *The Bible: Authorised King James Version* (Middlesex: Penguin Classics, 2006).
3. Hegel, "Architectural Works built for National Unification", *Aesthetics*, 638.

wer of Babel
mmunity
chitecture
aradox
ialectics
nguage

In this article I will argue that the choice of Babel as an exemplary symbol of national unity is emblematic of the difficulty that Hegel's unifying philosophical system presents for understanding community. This problem is structural, deriving from the essentially architectonic logic of dialectics, and connected to language at a fundamental level. This article excavates the uncertain foundations of the dialectic, calling into question the integrity of Hegel's system. In place of the dialectical structure, an 'anarchitectural' space will be proposed as the ground of community.[4] This reorientation suggests that the dialectical *telos*, like the Babylonian tower, is constitutively incomplete and reveals an intrinsic opacity to language. As such, Babel is shown to be an appropriate symbol for community ~ not for its unifying function, but because of its impossibility as a project, and the failure of communication that it represents.

In his *Aesthetics*, Hegel proposes that symbolic architecture is the origin of art ~ both historically, as the first kind of art that came into realisation, and philosophically, as the necessary first step in the conceptual development of the aesthetics *telos*.[5] He proposes that "the primary and original need of art is that an idea or thought generated by the spirit shall be produced by man as his own work and presented by him, just as in a language there are ideas which man communicates as such and makes intelligible to others."[6]

But where language communicates at the level of the sign, in which meaning is external and arbitrary in relation to the material form of the expression, Hegel argues that art has a sensuous presence that corresponds to its meaning.[7] This correspondence between essence and appearance defines the symbol, which "is no purely arbitrary sign, but a sign which in its externality comprises in itself at the same time the content of the idea which it brings into appearance."[8] Art consists precisely in this kinship of meaning and shape. It is therefore able to make visible essential thoughts that are *universal* in nature.

The symbolic names the first of three aesthetic moments, which each of the five particular arts passes through in the development of aesthetics. Through the dialectical movement of the Aufhebung, the symbolic is

---

4. This article is extracted from my doctoral research, which is concerned with articulating a non-essential ontology of community. I use the term 'anarchitectural' in two complimentary senses: firstly, to evoke a construction that is *anarchic* ~ implying a lack of centre or origin, as well as something of the political meaning of 'anarchy'; secondly, the word can be read as *ana-architectural*, by which I mean to indicate the return to a state prior to the architectonic logic of identity thinking, from where the ground of community can be thought anew. This is related to Heidegger's claim that metaphysical thought is built on a "groundless ground". cf. Martin Heidegger, *Identity and Difference*, trans Joan Stambaugh (New York: Harper & Row, 1969).

5. Hegel, "Independent or Symbolic Architecture", *Aesthetics*, 630.

6. Hegel, "Independent or Symbolic Architecture", *Aesthetics*, 635.

7. Ibid.

8. Hegel, "The Symbolic Form of Art" *Aesthetics*, 305.

superseded by the classical and then the romantic: first in architecture, then in sculpture, painting, music and poetry. The telos reaches its completion when all of these sensuous forms of art are sublated by aesthetics itself ~ that is, by philosophical reflection about art. As such, art is incorporated into spirit as it progresses to fully-formed Universal Reason.[9]

Being a linear unfolding, every *telos* must have a beginning, and this beginning has an essential correspondence with its end. The movement of the *Aufhebung* preserves what it supersedes, allowing the origin to reappear as a foundation in each successive stage of dialectical development. So Hegel's choice to put architecture at the origin reveals much about the nature of the system as a whole. I say 'choice', because in spite of certain initial claims, the text suggests that the identity between the historical beginning and the conceptual origin of art are not self-evident. Directly after stating that architecture's priority in the sequence is not only determined by the nature of art, but also because "it comes first in the existence of art in the world", Hegel seems to disavow this 'fact', claiming that "we must throughout exclude [...] the empirical facts of history".[10] Instead, what he wishes to demonstrate is the conceptual or essential nature of art, and Hegel proposes that "the first task of art consists in giving shape to what is objective in itself."[11] Strikingly, and in line with Denis Hollier's remarks on architecture's inaugural value for aesthetics as a whole, we find the reverse is true. Hollier writes, "instead of a serenely confident description of his object, we find the anxiety of someone attempting to grasp at an object that is elusive."[12]

First, Hegel identifies "the earliest beginnings of architecture, the first things that can be accepted as its commencement, [as being] a hut as a human dwelling, and a temple as an enclosure for the god and his community."[13] But he then rejects these structures as the origin of *aesthetics* because,

9. Hegel describes the process whereby the subject accedes to Universal Reason in the *Phenomenology*. Art is linked to religion as it plays a role in the development of spirit, but along with all sensuous experience it is eventually superseded by knowledge in its pure / total form. cf. G. W. F. Hegel, "Religion in the form of Art" and "The Revealed Religion", *The Phenomenology of Spirit*, trans A.V. Miller (Oxford: Oxford University Press, 1979), 424-479.

10. Hegel, "Independent or Symbolic Architecture", 630.

11. Hegel, "Independent or Symbolic Architecture", *Aesthetics*, 631.

12. Denis Hollier, *Against Architecture, the Writings of Georges Bataille*, trans Betsy Wing (Cambridge MA: MIT Press, 1989), 5. Hollier proposes that resistance to "architecture", which names an ordering and hence dominating form of logic, functions as an organising thread that runs through Bataille's oeuvre, and I should acknowledge Bataille's influence in this work. However, my challenge to the totalising claims of the Hegelian dialectic differs from Bataille's due to varying ontological approaches. Bataille breaches the totality by posing a question ('why?') after the completion of the telos, whereas I am claiming that the dialectic is always already incomplete from the beginning, because of the uncertain foundations on which it is built. cf. Georges Bataille, "Hegel", *Inner Experience*, trans Leslie Anne Boldt (Albany: State University of New York Press, 1988), 108-111.

13. Hegel, "Independent or Symbolic Architecture", *Aesthetics*, 631.

"such erections are mere *means*, presupposing a purpose external to them."[14] Whereas art is a pertinent concept only for objects that have as their end the manifestation of the idea of beauty. However, the distinction between internality and externality, means and ends, is continually called into question throughout this foundational section of the text.

In order to find the beginnings of aesthetics Hegel looks for examples of buildings that are pure symbols, independent of any external aims or needs (in other words, of any usefulness), those which stand "like works of sculpture, and which carry their meaning in themselves."[15] One might ask what exactly differentiates a 'building' that has no practical use from a 'work of sculpture'. Hegel's text does not make this entirely clear. Sculpture follows after architecture in the aesthetic *telos*, but serves as a controlling model for it. Hollier points out that "this paradoxical situation [leads] Hegel to define, contrary to any proper hierarchy, architecture, the first of arts, as a type of the second, sculpture".[16]

However, as already observed, the *telos* must have a beginning, and if the first task of art is to give shape to what is objective, then this beginning must be an object. The object that Hegel identifies as the originary type of symbolic architecture is a work built for national unification: "the *primary* purpose behind explicitly independent buildings is only the erection of something which is a unifying point for a nation or nations, a place where they assemble."[17] And the example he gives as the very first of such structures is the biblical story of the Tower of Babylonia, or Babel.[18] The Tower of Babel is distinguished from utilitarian architecture by the fact that it is a solid structure without an internal cavity, so there is no possibility of the 'external aims or needs' which most buildings are mediated by penetrating into the inside. The structure is able to function ideologically as a pure symbol because its solidity gives it a homogeneous self-presence, ensuring that there is no risk of confusion between forms, between interiority and exteriority.[19]

---

14. Ibid.

15. Hegel, "Independent or Symbolic Architecture", *Aesthetics*, 632.

16. Hollier, 8.

17. Hegel, "Independent or Symbolic Architecture", *Aesthetics*, 637.

18. Hegel, "Architectural Works built for National Unification", 638-9.

19. Hollier, 9. A relation can be seen between the homogeneous self-presence of the architectural symbol and the structure of the metaphysical subject. Jean-Luc Nancy proposes that thinking in terms of the subject as interiority is what thwarts a thinking of community, suggesting instead that beings be thought as surfaces that are constituted as they are exposed to the outside. Although he does not discuss architecture in this context, Nancy's ontology is based on a topological spatiality which does not conform to the euclidean logic on which architecture is based, thus implying the kind of anarchitectural ground that I am proposing here. cf. Jean-Luc-Nancy, *The Inoperative Community*, edited Peter Connor (Minneapolis: University of Minnesota Press, 1991), 1-42.

But on another level, the separation of interiority from exteriority is not so simple. If the primary purpose of the Tower, and structures like it, is to function as a place of assembly, this would seem to make them precisely a means to an end which is external to that of beauty. And this was the very reason that the hut and the temple were disqualified from being categorised as aesthetic objects. The aim of constituting human community seems to take precedence over the properly aesthetic aspect of the symbol, even in the chapter in which Hegel describes what corresponds to the purest form of symbolism in art.[20] Indeed, as Hollier observes "[t]he word 'symbolic' is scarcely used."[21] The fact that community predominates over the symbol in this discussion emphasises the importance of sociality in Hegel's ideas about Reason. If community is the purpose of the architectural symbol this is because, for Hegel, it is only in the life of a *people* or *nation* that self-conscious Reason's actualisation (the result of the *telos*) has its reality.[22] But the question remains as to the value of the architectural symbol as a purely aesthetic object.

At the opening of the section entitled "Architectural Works built for National Unification", Hegel cites Goethe, who says that "[w]hat is holy" is "[w]hat links many souls together".[23] And Hegel suggests that "the holy, with the aim of this concord, and as this concord, [is] the first content of independent architecture."[24] Which is to say that 'holy concord' is both the aim of the architecture and what it already contains, indicating some confusion, or at least conflation, between present and future, between what *is* and what *will be*. And this confusion continues throughout the section on symbolic architecture, the result of the process is presupposed as a requirement for its beginning. This produces a kind of circular agitation, which is what makes it so difficult for Hegel to locate a stable origin. This circularity, I would argue, is the sort of movement that is generated by a paradox ~ which is quite different from a contradiction. All of which suggests that the paradox, rather than dialectical negation serves as a foundation for this architecture.[25]

Hegel says that the Tower of Babel, his first actual example of independent architecture, "was built in common, and the aim and content of the work was

20. Hegel, "Independent or Symbolic Architecture", *Aesthetics*, 635-659.

21. Hollier, 11.

22. Hegel, Phenomenology of Spirit, § 350, 212.

23. Hegel, "Architectural Works built for National Unification", *Aesthetics*, 638.

24. Ibid.

25. For Deleuze, the paradox forms the ground of sense. In contrast to the negativity of Hegelian contradiction, he proposes that sense is produced in the affirmation of a positive distance, which is characteristic of the surface, not of depth. cf. Gilles Deleuze, *The Logic of Sense*, trans Mark Lester. (London / New York: Continuum, 2004), 197. This surface is topological, hence Deleuzian sense can be related to the ontological sociality proposed by Nancy (Supra n. 19). The paradox, as that which, "destroys good sense as the only direction, but is also that which destroys common sense as the assignation of fixed identities", always implies an anarchitectural spatiality. (Deleuze, *Negatiations*, 5).

at the same time the community of those who constructed it."[26] Now, in order for this project to commence, to be built 'in common', there must already be a social bond, the foundation of which, Hegel tells us, had already superseded unification on patriarchal lines.[27] This means that a social unity, which results from familial ties being sublated into a wider whole, exists prior to the architectural work of National Unification. Hegel offers no account of how the "purely family unity [that] has already been superseded" itself came into being ~ patriarchal unification is presupposed. But if the family unit comprises a number of individual subjects fused into a greater whole, then it seems that (at least) two levels of communal unification have already been passed through prior to the commencement of the architectural project. Which suggests a certain complexity in the sociality that is a prerequisite for the architectural work.

All of this means that community precedes nation, and indeed serves as its ground. What the architectural work builds onto this communal ground is a symbol, which represents the identity of the nation. So architecture brings a pre-existing, intuitive communal bond into the realm of representation, of language. This association between architecture and language is not unique to Hegel ~ structural linguistics, for example, uses an architectural vocabulary to explain the workings of language. In this sense, linguistics seems to owe a debt of foundation to architecture. Indeed, as Hollier comments, "Viollet-le-Duc's *Dictionnaire de l'architecture Française* followed a structuralist analytical method (one since developed by Saussure and the linguists) before the term was invented."[28] Similarly, for Jacques Lacan, it is an edifice that, "remind[s] us of what distinguishes architecture from building: namely, a logical power that governs the architecture beyond what the building allows for by way of possible utilization."[29] Architecture, then, as distinct from mere building, has a logical power ~ the power of the logos ~ which governs language as such, and systems more generally. Consequently, as Hollier observes:

> "There is no way to describe a system without resorting to a vocabulary of architecture. When structure defines the general form of legibility, nothing becomes legible unless it is submitted to the architectural grid. Architecture under these conditions becomes archistructure,

26. Hegel, "Architectural Works built for National Unification", *Aesthetics*, 638.
27. Ibid.
28. Hollier, 32.
29. Jacques Lacan, *Écrits*, trans Bruce Fink (New York / London: W. W. Norton & Co., 2006), [698] 586.

the system of systems. The keystone of systematicity in general, it organizes the concord of languages and guarantees universal legibility."[30]

And yet, returning again to the beginning ~ this time, to the account of the Babylonian tower in Genesis ~ the foundational position of architecture in relation to language is, once again, called into question. Because *before* the inaugural architectural project commenced, as the Bible tells us:

> "[...] the whole earth was of one language, and of one speech. [...] And they said, Go to, let us build us a city and a tower, whose top may reach unto heaven; and let us make us a name, lest we be scattered abroad across the face of the whole earth."[31]

Universal legibility and concord of language were, it seems, already in existence prior to the originary work of architecture. Architecture comes after language. What the edifice aimed to create was not language-in-general, but 'a name' ~ an identity. Hegel suggests that the product of building this symbol of identity was to be a bond that linked the workers together "as we are linked together by manners, customs, and the legal constitution of the state".[32] But is language not the condition that allows manners, customs and legal structures to be instituted (not to mention the expression of identity)? If so, the community was already unified by its shared language; indeed it must have been, or the tower would never have been built. Which makes Babel a paradoxical symbol for unity, if one considers the end of the tale (and in a *telos* the meaning is always to be found as / at the end):

> "And the LORD said, Behold, the people is one, and they have all one language; and this they begin to do: and now nothing will be restrained from them, which they have imagined to do.
>
> Go to, let us go down, and there confound their language, that they may not understand one another's speech.
>
> So the LORD scattered them abroad from thence upon the face of all the earth."[33]

---

30. Hollier, 33.
31. "Genesis", 11:1, 11:4, *The Bible*, 2006.
32. Hegel, 'Architectural Works built for National Unification', *Aesthetics*, 638.
33. Genesis, 11:6-8, *The Bible*, 2006.

Far from organizing concord and legibility, the so-called inaugural architectural work provoked an irreparable fragmentation in a people that had formerly been united by their shared language. This confounding of language, the medium of rational discourse, means that far from being a symbol of unity, Babel represents the origin of opacity and confusion in communication, which would seem to cause disjunction in the community.

Hegel attributes the failure of the tower to unify the people to the fact that it was only in an external way that it was able to express what is holy, that it could only hint at the social bond. Here again, he contradicts himself, if we recall that earlier, the symbol was defined as a sign in which the sensuous manifestation corresponds with the essential idea that it represents. Time and again, the foundation seems to unwork itself, and I argue that Hegel's difficulty in identifying the architectural object, and establishing its originary position, derives from a blind-spot in the architectonic logic of his own edifice ~ that is, the dialectical *telos* as a hierarchical and totalising system. And this blind-spot, in turn, makes it impossible for him to think community as such.

The problem is that Hegel wants to define community according to what comes after it in the teleological process ~ the nation, unified by an identity concept that is constituted through the work of construction, and manifested as an architectural symbol. But community, as that which necessarily precedes this process, is neither *a work*, nor an identity concept. Unable to conceptualise this prior state of sociality in its complexity, because it doesn't conform to the structural logic of his system, Hegel can only project a symbolic meaning backwards onto it, designating it as origin with hindsight. By attributing architecture with the status of origin, Hegel conceals what came before it ~ which would be the beginning, properly speaking; the same beginning that Hegel seems unable to locate. And so community is excluded from architectural space, and remains an excess in relation to the dialectic, consigned to an exteriority that precedes the space of representation.

All of this means that Hegel is unable to see the foundation on which his own, dialectical edifice is built: this exteriority, which is 'anarchitectural' in nature ~ de-centred and structured according to a spatial logic that is entirely heterogeneous to the Euclidean principles on which architecture is based. This anarchic space, which forms the groundless ground of the system, poses a threat to the integrity of the edifice and must remain excluded, lest it cause the structure to unravel. And so the dialectic, which is claimed to accede to a total Knowledge from which nothing is excluded, is constitutively incomplete.

In this sense, the Hegelian edifice resembles the Tower of Babel, as a folly that could never have been completed ~ a work that attempted to unite the people by transcending the horizontality of the mortal world and making them equal with God, building a route to transcendence in bricks and mortar. Hegel, too, claims to have conceived a system, an architecture, that can reach the height of transcendence, an Absolute Knowledge that could be characterised as divine. In this architectonic system language is presented as a transparent medium that is able to communicate all ideas. But as long as the anarchitectural ground is obscured by the assumed completeness of the structure, there remains an opacity at the root of communication. The same opacity of language inaugurated by the communal project of the Tower. On a certain level, community is nothing other than this failure of communication, the excess that cannot be incorporated by the structure that is dependent on it. So the myth of Babel can be seen as a symbol, not of unity, but of the founding of community through the confounding of tongues.

Hannah Lammin

Mimetic Rationality:

Abstract: This work is an engagement with the experiential. Mimesis and the work of Theodor Adorno was always already going to be just an occasion for a presumptive use value rather than another straw exchange for those who would break a camel's back. The piece asks questions after the nature of 'what in', 'how and why is' the lead voice in written work is to be sanctified and thereafter dictates its own amendment to the puzzle. The absent voice (Pharmakos) could be said to be reiterating earlier attempts at a merger of the Derridian and Adornian into a regulative orthodoxy. Nothing could be further from the case. The relational tensors mask a radical orthodoxy, a mimetic specification before judgement and understanding, becomes presence in absence. The development of forms leads to this exchange / merger of the organic with the inorganic. And all this set against the injunction forbidding the pouring of new wine into old bottles.

The developmental process that Hegel describes, the sublation of one nature by another nature qualified by its fit to the functional context of society, the movement from awakening consciousness to social and institutional constructs (family, school, church, and state, that kind of thing but also friendship, shared interests, civility, etc.,) echoes the more anthropological, speculative and productive history of mimesis and rationality found within Theodor Adorno and Max Horkheimer's *Dialectic of Enlightenment*, which posits three phases in the development of mimesis and rationality: the pre-historical, the magical, and the historical.[1] At the earliest phase there is an adaptation to environment, a self-conscious following of the course of nature carried out in order to avoid the contingency and excesses of the world. In the magical phase there is developed an organized control of mimesis. Confrontations with what is ordered as amorphous and immediate nature, bolster a mimetic taboo against the immediate, sensed. The taboo is maintained and developed by a dictatorial minority with fatal means that projects Stoic virtues as virtuous nature. Since the mimetic taboo art became the organ of mimesis. Art now defines an area tolerantly reserved for mimesis.[2]

Adaptation to nature, to the seasons, migration of animals, etc., a veritable becoming other, is an aspect of archaic mimesis adaptation to the inanimate and inorganic another. Mimesis of inorganic nature as a way to

1. Theodor Adorno and Max Horkheimer, *Dialectic of Enlightenment*, trans John Cumming, (London: Verso, 1997).

2. Adorno and Horkheimer, Dialectic of Enlightenment, 180. Cf. Theodor Adorno. "Expression and Dissonance," *Aesthetic Theory*, trans Robert Hullot-Kentor, (United States of America: The Athlone Press, 1997), 110. 'Mimetic comportment ~ an attitude towards reality distinct from the fixed antithesis of subject and object ~ is seized in art ~ the organ of mimesis since the mimetic taboo ~ by semblance and, as the complement to the autonomy of form, becomes its bearer.'

periential
imesis
armakos
lational tensors
dividualism
gative dialectics
d bottles
ganic & inorganic mergers

escape the terrors of nature, a nature from which the animate self with no little effort had recently estranged itself is in aspect, an adaptation to death (implying a reversion of the self to a mere state of nature).[3] Playing dead, hiding out of terror, incorporating death into life, are ways of avoiding external confrontation. This becomes much more important in the mythical / magical mimetic phase where the notion of sacrifice is advanced (the present moment to the future). This contains a form of rationality whereby prescriptive scenarios, rites, rituals, myths, and sacrifices are performed in the belief that nature will look favourably upon human goals. In performance or enactment something is consummated, but also something new / addendum can be generated. The Shaman copies something in the future. What we have come to know as art has its roots here in the magical, and intentionally or not and to a greater or lesser extent it retains the power of prescription. Once the doubling of nature becomes intentional then self-empowerment is optimized through a mode of rational interaction. Mimesis of the hardened and estranged is reproduction of an earlier state: adaptation is repeated adaptation.

Each time a conscious decision is made it more or less reflects the moments it consistently has access to. All productive thought that does not simply reconstruct or recapitulate to what has come before and wants to gain knowledge of something without covering categories has to surrender to it without reservation. This itself is not a recipe for success. To succeed the knowledge that is actualised through immersion in the object would have to potentiate theory, ready and waiting however concealed with sudden flashes of illumination. Philosophical knowledge begins where it opens up what traditional thought considers opaque, impenetrable and individual. "For the right practice and for the good itself, there is really no other authority than the most advanced state of theory."[4]

Theory prevents the mind from becoming an absolute. Critical self-reflection keeps the subject open, keeps it from building walls between itself and its object, from constricting the abundance of ways to react. The mobility of consciousness, one of its best features, points to a double mode of conduct: On the one hand an immanent dialectical process that criticizes the system and recalls what would be outside of it, and on the other, free unbound, unregimented thought that allows us to step outside of the dialectic. Both aspects of consciousness are linked by the non-compromising and critical attitudes they take to each other.[5] Their elective affinity lies in the fact that,

---

3. Adorno and Horkheimer, *Dialectic of Enlightenment*, 31.
4. Theodor Adorno, *Negative Dialectics*, trans E.B Ashton, (Great Britain: Routledge, 1996), 242.
5. Adorno, *Negative Dialectics*, 31.

the force that liberates the dialectical movement in cognition is the very same that rebels against the system.

Whatever subjectively 'is' includes an objectivity that has yet to be established. The element of objective reason internal to subjective reason, the *ratio* that transcends its subjective place holders is rational identity. Its moment of universality, linked to the realm of pure purpose, cannot be divorced from a plethora of drives, natures, mortalities, etc. The most subjective, naïve immediacy, eludes for a brief spell the interventionist intentions of the subject and presents us with an opportunity to see something as it really is.[6] However the immediacy of insight, the receptivity within synthesizing consciousness is a phenomenon not to be denied. It gives rise in the judgement to a recognition and configuration of both example and comparison. Without the moment of insight the particular could not be the universal. It is only its hypostasis that is to be denied.

In terms of essence the permanent exercise of caution in both directions, the implicit and the explicit, points to the non-dimensional in Being. Being is compressed into a point. As a procedure this has its *fundament in re.* Categorical vision, the growing awareness of a concept, must have a corresponding moment beyond the sensory matter. Spontaneous thoughts are phenomenon. Categorical vision has an immediacy that resembles visuality, this makes it, arguably, a self-adjustment rather than an activity. Traditional epistemology knew this as a synthesis, as categorically constituted facts. The factual moment isolated and hypostatized, a protest against the split between concept and entity, ceases to be a moment and becomes a thing: the separation and reduction of phenomenal and spontaneous thought to a thought deemed both scientific and necessary. Categorical vision, despite its fallibility, contributes to the understanding of the thing itself not its classification. That mental facts can be purely described, isolated, accepted as what they claim to be is both a dogma and a demand.[7]

The view of sensory things in their not being absolute or irrefutable corresponds to a moment of direct vision. What is astir in this seemingly directness of the given is the experience, the congealed transmission, of what has come to be. The sense of evolved objectivity in things that supposedly merely are, is an awareness of the break between a things identity and its concept: "in this respect essence perception is close to allegorical

6. Cf. Adorno, *Negative Dialectics*, 38-40. "To receive something as it is offered at a time, dispensing with reflection, is potentially always tantamount to recognizing it the way it is; virtually all thoughts, on the other hand, cause a negative motion.[...] The most subjective, the immediate datum, eludes the subject's interventions. Yet such immediate consciousness is neither consciously maintainable nor downright positive."

7. Adorno, *Negative Dialectics*, 81.

consciousness."[8] This allows for a binding physiognomy of the mind, a physiognomic flash, or essence perception that does not simply attribute mental objectivity to projections of a contemplating subject.[9]

As the physiological primordial form of spirit, mimesis and its modification is the process whereby reason sets itself up as the psychologically real self, the I of self-consciousness and self-preservation. "In the constitution of the ego reflective mimesis becomes controlled reflection. 'Recognition in the concept,' the absorption of the different by the same, takes the place of physical adaptation to nature."[10] As the non-identical within the rational, mimesis expresses a refusal to reflect the categorizing order, it splits asunder the idea of a rationalisation of reason calling everything to account from the preserve of a single aspect viewpoint. The substance of a changed philosophy would lie in the diversity of the objects that impinge upon it and of the objects it seeks, a diversity not wrought by any schema. "To those objects philosophy would truly give itself rather than use them as a mirror in which to reread itself, mistaking its own image for concretion."[11]

Objects that impinge on philosophy: a positive dialectics uses them as a mirror in which to reread itself, mistaking its own image and power of representation as guarantee for concretion. The capacity for representation (*Vorstellung*) is both progressive and regressive: the capacity of representation is the measure of domination and in performance domination is the most powerful thing that can be represented. Adaptation to the power of progress involves the progress of power in its capacity for representation. For the dominant to survive it must not be tempted by that which is unrepeatable. The fixed order of time, the three fold schema of past, present and future, is intended to free the present from the clutches of the past. The power of the past is referred behind the absolute barrier of the unrepeatable.[12] Nevertheless, the past is placed at the disposal of the present as practicable knowledge. The practical by directly invoking the recent past with the irresistible promise of pleasure turns the temptation of self-abandonment into a mere object of contemplation: becomes art.

"The subjective impulse that registers what is to be done is the appearance of something objective transpiring back of this impulse, the

8. Adorno and Horkheimer, *Dialectic of Enlightenment*, 82.

9. See for example where they write: "Essence perception is our word for the physiognomic view of mental facts-a legitimate view because things of the mind are not constituted by the cognitive intentionality of consciousness but are based objectively, far beyond the individual author, on the collective life of the mind, in accordance with its immanent laws.", 82.

10. Adorno and Horkheimer, *Dialectic of Enlightenment*, 181.

11. Adorno, *Negative Dialectics*, 13.

12. Adorno and Horkheimer, *Dialectic of Enlightenment*, 32-33.

development of productive forces, which art in its innermost has in common with society and at the same time opposes through its own development. In art, development has multiple meanings".[13]

The absorption of art alien techniques external to art but originating in society is one of art's developing means, and part of its autarchy. In practice impulses must be doggedly sublimated in an additional effort, an addendum, which must ignore the drive that impels to diversion. But all unification remains deception and so thought becomes illusionary wherever it seeks to deny its divisive / decisive function. As a specific undertaking integration binds the centrifugal counter-forces, absorbs the manifold and creates abstract unity by removing the antithetical element, by virtue of which the unity came to be in the first place. Released from the empirical as from the totality of the heteronomous subjective pleasure, the happiness in artworks, would be the feeling of holding firm.[14] Art appeases the compulsion to rescue the past as something living. Instead of using the past as the material of progress art appertains to a presentation of past life which is not cognition. This separates it from social practice which merely tolerates art as it tolerates pleasure.[15]

The transposition of impulses, the plenipotentiary in the aesthetic continuum of extra-aesthetic nature, is in effect a claim that by virtue of the artistic integration the impulses are no longer incarnate as the extra-aesthetic nature's afterimage. Aesthetic structures create a continuum that is totally spirit. In that way they become the semblance of a blocked being-in-itself in whose reality the intentions of the subject would be fulfilled and extinguished.[16] Art develops this act through the work that, mollifying the pain, modifies mimesis through imagination.

The subject as the only adequate instrument of expression is itself mediated. The impulses are those of the subject and yet participating in the integrative power of the ego they nevertheless remain nonidentical with respect to the ego formation. Even though it resembles the subject the expressed is the nonsubjective in the subject. Expression is a priori imitation that having been objectified endures. The expression of artworks is not so much the subject's expression as its copy.

"Expression, by which nature seeps most deeply into art, is at the same time what is not literally nature, a memento of what expression itself is not, of what could not have become concrete except through the *how* of that expression."[17]

13. Adorno, *Aesthetic Theory*, 192.
14. Adorno, *Aesthetic Theory*. 15.
15. Adorno and Horkheimer, *Dialectic of Enlightenment*, 32.
16. Adorno, *Aesthetic Theory*, 113.
17. Adorno, *Aesthetic Theory*. 113-114.

With regards to the question of *how* (of expression) the key position for the subject in cognition is experience, and not the constituent form. Knowledge steps up and comes close where the subject as agent and entrusting itself to its own experiences acts, rendering the veil it weaves about the object without anxiety. For example, the fact that music as a whole has its source in the collective practices of cult and dance is no mere point of departure. The historical source remains the unique sensory subjective impulse of music, something that continues to weave its spell on the collective practice.

The more art expels the pre-established the more it is thrown back on the dimensionless point of pure subjectivity. In art's secularization of transcendence, the tendency of the subjective point to expel the pre-established leads to an absence of social resonance, a contraction of the accessible. The resulting impoverished powerless gesture, the scream of the destitute, is a confession concerning the impossibility of artistic objectivation: a postulate common to all artistic manifestations. The aesthetic concept of anti-art anticipates this dialectic and constantly tries to abrogate its postulate. The implication being that art must go beyond its own concept in order to remain faithful to that concept.[18]

Mark Walker

---

18. Adorno, *Aesthetic Theory*, 30.

Intimate Strategies:

Abstract: Morton insists that ecology requires intimacy between ecosystems and organisms, living and non-living entities. Paradoxically, Morton suggests that intimacy incurs a sense of strangeness between things. As a predecessor of queer theory, Foucault commends human intimacy as an act of resistance against institutionalized sexuality. Such intimacy, Foucault suggests, enhances our sense of strangeness to ourselves. I not only grant that queer theory and ecology share an emphasis on intimacy but I argue this intimacy must be defined as the transmutation of distance, a drawing close that simultaneously estranges. Through Bachelard, I link this account to a poetics of intimate space.

Although a certain environmental philosophy inflected with queer theory has been alive for over a decade now, and far longer if one were to count its early development within ecofeminism, the term 'queer ecology' still strikes many as fundamentally awkward and perhaps even perverse. What does a queer theory, for which Medusa represents the perils of phallogocentrism, have to do with an ecology, which would rather just talk about snakes? And what does an ecology, which is pre-eminently concerned with the planet's survival, have to do with a strand of queer theory, which can hardly give the future a second glance?[1] On the face of it, these disciplines share very little. Ecology and queer theory appear to be but distant cousins. No doubt this is one of the reasons the queer ecological movement has been called a "Frankensteinian meme splice."[2] It is a little incongruous and slightly monstrous.

Despite the apparent monstrosity of a discipline like queer ecology, however, many scholars have developed convincing accounts of the co-reverberations between queer theory and ecology. This work is being done in and across a number of fields, including biology, literary criticism, and cultural studies.[3] These accounts, moreover, are far from mere intellectual experiments. In their introduction to *Queer Ecologies: Sex, Nature, Politics, Desire*,[4]

1. See Lee Edelman's *No Future* (Durham: Duke University Press, 2004), and the long tradition of responses to it.

2. Timothy Morton, "Queer Ecology", *Publication of the Modern Languages Association* (PMLA), 125, no. 2 (2010): 273.

3. See, for example, Robert Azzarello, *Queer Environmentality: Ecology, Evolution, and Sexuality in American Literature*, (Farnham: Ashgate, 2012); Bruce Bagemihl, *Biological Exuberance: Animal Homosexuality and Natural Diversity*, (New York: St. Martin's Press, 1999); Joan Roughgarden, *Evolution's Rainbow: Diversity, Gender, and Sexuality in Nature and People* (Berkeley: University of California Press, 2009); Nicole Seymour, *Strange Natures: Futurity, Empathy, and the Queer Ecological Imagination*, (Champaign: University of Illinois Press, 2013); and Noel Sturgeon, *Environmentalism in Popular Culture: Gender, Race, Sexuality, and the Politics of the Natural*, (Tucson: University of Arizona Press, 2008).

4. Catriona Sandilands and Bruce Erickson, *Queer Ecologies: Sex, Nature, Politics, Desire*, (Bloomington: Indiana University Press, 2010).

orton
ucault
chelard
sistance
eer ecology
rangeness
ing and non-living ecologies
stitutionalised sexuality

Catriona Sandilands and Bruce Erickson offer a genealogy of the discipline; that is, they trace several ways queer theory and ecology have been not only theoretically co-considered, but historically intertwined. Sandilands and Erickson observe, for instance, that the discourses of sex and the discourses of nature have consistently informed one another. One can think, most basically, of Darwin and Krafft-Ebing. They also, however, mark that the construction of natural spaces ~ like parks, camping sites, forest preserves, wilderness areas, etc. ~ has entailed a concomitant construction of sexuality in space. By tracing these connections, Sandilands and Erickson intimate that queer ecology is a necessary analysis of the historical and material overlap between nature and sex. In this essay, I contribute to this work of identifying the theoretical basis of queer ecology. I analyse two accounts which suggest that queer theory and ecology are commensurate insofar as they both appeal to a radical intimacy between entities. First, I consider Timothy Morton's account of ecology, which insists that ecology appeals to a structural intimacy one also finds in queer theory. Morton then defines intimacy as the breakdown of binaries by which we can experience the neighbour as stranger. Second, I consider one of the grounding stories of queer theory: Michel Foucault's account of sexuality. He suggests that, in the 19th century, both sexuality and the environment became special objects of governmentality. He claims that institutionalized sexuality ~ and by implication, institutionalized environmentalism ~ can be resisted through the exercise of intimacy. In the context of sexuality, Foucault defines intimacy as a physicality by which we can experience ourselves as stranger. Based on Morton and Foucault's accounts, I theorize that ecological and queer theoretical intimacy is the transmutation of distance or the intimate nearing that is also a strange distancing. Queer ecology, then, is a discipline concerned with what one might call the poetics of intimate / uncanny space. I then develop this poetics with reference to the work of Gaston Bachelard, who suggests, in *The Poetics of Space*, that intimate space collapses and expands in a spiral. Finally, I draw implications for the work of interdisciplinarity, whether as queer ecology or otherwise.

Ecology as Intimacy

Timothy Morton, author of *Ecology without Nature* and *The Ecological Thought*, argues for the necessity of queer ecology. His defence is not historical in nature, but rather structural. In "Queer Ecology," Morton suggests that the mechanics by which ecology and queer theory function, the rhetoric on which they both rely, and indeed the very logic upon which they both rest, have one thing in common: an appeal to *intimacy*. He argues that both disciplines appeal to an intimacy across and against boundaries, under the conviction that the great distance between you and me, between here and there, between that one and this one is just an illusion that we can re-imagine over and over again. Ecology, Morton writes, "demands intimacies with other beings that queer theory also demands, in another key."[5]

In keeping with his structural analysis, Morton elucidates this shared demand for intimacy by first detailing the theoretical 'death of nature' and then developing its epistemological and ethical implications. He encapsulate these implications in two elemental concepts: the 'mesh' and the 'strange stranger.' Throughout, Morton builds his account of intimacy primarily with reference to ecology, and thereby leaves somewhat vague the content and extent of answering reverberations in queer theory.

Although Morton marks the death of nature in "Queer Ecology," he develops it at much greater length in *Ecology without Nature*. There, Morton heralds the death of nature specifically as the demise of a nature conceived of as outside, over there, transcendent and independent of human existence. It is Morton's suspicion that the 'late' transcendent nature comes too quickly to the aid of empty decrees about what is and isn't natural, what is and isn't 'born this way.' But it also never quite arrives up against or inside human entities enough to make what appears natural an utter mystery, or what appears inborn to be still quite unknown. Because the concept of nature thus undergirds untenable claims of strict taxonomy, it necessarily defies relationality and defeats, from the outset, the sort of being-with requisite for ecological ethics. Thankfully, for Morton, that concept is itself untenable in light of an increasingly intimate world.

In place of a dead nature, Morton proposes, in *The Ecological Thought*, something called the 'mesh.' Think of chainmail or fishnets. A mesh in this sense is composed of both threads and holes. Morton suggests that this observation is born out etymologically, with 'mesh' having both the words 'mass' and 'mask' in its history.[6] Mesh, then, would simultaneously signify densely networked threads and the deceptive, or perhaps seductive, spaces between them. For Morton, the illusion of nature, which stands aloof from humans and non-living things alike, must be replaced by the reality of a mesh: the broad interconnection of the living and the dead, presence and absence. This mesh is marked by two things. First, the mesh involves everything that exists. If there is no outside, then everything is here. "All life forms," he writes, "are the mesh," but "so are all the dead ones, as are their habitats, which are

5. Morton, "Queer Ecology," 273. See also: Timothy Morton, *Ecology without Nature* (Harvard: Harvard University Press, 2007), 13.

6. According to the Oxford English Dictionary, this is one of two possible etymologies. See further: *The Concise Oxford English Dictionary, Main Edition*, (Oxford: Oxford University Press, 2011), 944.

also made up of living and non-living beings."[7] Second, the mesh entails the blurring of everything that exists. It is "a non-totalizable, open-ended concatenation of interrelations that blur and confound boundaries at any practical level."[8] What was once nature over there is now an endlessly muddied mesh right here.

If all that exists, exists in a mesh, then certainly the so-called 'other' ~ the other outside, over there, transcendent and independent of the self ~ must have gone the way of nature. Instead of selves and others, each existent exists in a sea of what Morton calls 'strange strangers.' The term 'strange stranger' is, as Morton states, "my bad translation of Derrida's *arrivant*."[9] Jacques Derrida's *arrivant*, in turn, is a term that signifies 'the one who comes.' Since the one who comes never actually arrives, the *arrivant* cannot be identified as either this sort of creature or that, human or non-human, alive or dead. Morton's 'strange stranger,' however, is already here, all around us. Nevertheless, it maintains the *arrivant's* sense of utter strangeness for at least two reasons. First, it is not me, or not just me, or not exactly me, and in this sense it will always be a stranger. Second, it is not itself, or not just itself, or not exactly itself, and in this sense it will always be strange. When one takes the mesh seriously, with all the interconnections and interdependence it requires, one realizes that things become at once less and more than they ever were before. The more of a mesh one has, the less one has ~ less substances, less bodies, less lines and identities, but also the more of everything in between and underneath. What could be stranger than that?

Morton's concepts of the 'mesh' and the 'strange stranger' have a direct bearing on ecological ethics. Contrary to the reigning call for inclusive ethics, Morton demands an ethics of intimacy. Under the old theory of nature, where the inside and the outside were carefully maintained, ethics meant enlarging the inside ~ including animals, farms, or variously excluded others within the circle of legitimized and legislated subjects. These subjects, however, maintained their own insides and outsides, so that ethics meant preserving a respectful distance between equal entities. Morton's mesh, however, messes with that. It demonstrates that distance itself has broken down; the outside and the inside are no longer traditionally distinguishable. In this state, "rather than a vision of inclusion," he writes, "we need a vision of intimacy:" an intimacy that "necessitates thinking and practicing weakness rather than mastery, fragmentariness rather than holism, and deconstructive tentativeness rather than aggressive assertion."[10]

7. Timothy Morton, *The Ecological Thought*, 29.
8. Morton, "Queer Ecology", 275-276.
9. Morton, "Queer Ecology", 277.
10. Morton, "Queer Ecology", 278.

Now, Morton's ultimate claim is that ecology and queer theory share a call to intimacy or a commitment to meshy strangeness. Morton's arguments from the side of queer theory, however, are all too brief. Here, I present them as schematically as possible. First, Morton claims that the death of nature entails the demise of the binary between nature and culture. As such, it also entails the demise of the correlative binaries of man and woman, masculine and feminine, heterosexual and homosexual. If the former cannot be held apart, neither can the latter.[11] The death of nature, then, must be consistent with, if not constitutive of, queer theory. Second, Morton glosses Judith Butler's theory of performativity, according to which gender is defined as a series of iterated signs. Morton then observes that DNA is equally iterative. If performativity, then, is the mark of the queer, and if DNA is performative, then DNA is queer. Thus, queer theory and ecology are concerned with the same objects.[12] Third, Morton mentions Darwin's argument that sexuality is attributable to sheer aesthetic display. Sexual overtures, whether officially queer or not queer, are merely the expression of pleasure and not the fulfilment of some innate demand for survival. If aesthetic pleasure is the mark of the queer, and if all sex is aesthetically driven, then all sex is queer.[13] Morton concludes that, "Ecology is queer theory and queer theory is ecology: queer ecology."[14]

By leaning in toward the mesh, or the 'is,' and away from the strange stranger, or the 'is not,' Morton's structural argument has certain limitations: 1) it obscures the historical vicissitudes to the relationship between nature and sex, and 2) it obscures the uncanniness that still separates queer theory from ecology. Thus, for instance, the way in which queer performativity is unique to queer theory and the divergent ways in which performativity may or may not have been discursively considered in evolutionary theory are passed over. I turn, therefore, to the work of Michel Foucault both to balance structural analysis with genealogy, and to further explore the claim that intimacy transmutes distance into meshy strangeness.

Queer Theory as Intimacy

Michel Foucault is widely considered to be at the root of queer theory, while his perhaps equally significant (if not extensive) contributions to ecological analysis have gone relatively unnoticed. Most introductions to queer theory mention

11. Morton, "Queer Ecology", 274.

12. As Morton says, in his "Queer Ecology", "DNA itself is performative [...] If you want a queer monument, look around you." 276.

13. As Morton clarifies, "Because Darwin reduces sexuality to sheer aesthetic display [his work] is as anti-homophobic as it is antiracist." 278.

14. Morton, "Queer Ecology", 281.

the significance of Foucault's *History of Sexuality*, especially its characterization of sexuality as a regime of power and knowledge.[15] Recently, Lynne Huffer has extended that debt to *History of Madness*, in which, as she argues, sexuality is cast as "a category of moral and political exclusion."[16] If, in some sense, queer theory is concerned with the resistance to institutionalized sexuality, then Foucault's diagnosis of that institutionalization is one of queer theory's beginnings. By no means, however, was Foucault solely concerned with sexuality. He was concerned more broadly with any instance of institutionalization. For this reason, several scholars have developed his much briefer analyses of the institution of nature, the governing of natural spaces, and environmental discourses.[17]

Here, I will trace Foucault's contribution to a theory of queer ecology, specifically one that resonates with Morton's account. First, I will review Foucault's history of natural science, wherein he demonstrates that the policing of sexuality and the policing of species are equally tied up in the 19th century turn to life-management or biopower. Then, I will mark Foucault's history of sexuality, where he proffers a resistant ethics of transformative intimacy.

By inference, I argue, the sort of intimacy that defeats the policing of sexuality must be related to the intimacy required by ecology. In this way, I conclude with a revised description of the sort of intimacy that anchors queer theory in ecology, and vice versa.

Throughout his histories of sexuality and natural science, Foucault is quite aware not only of the length of these histories but also of the divergent ways in which 'sex' and 'the environment' have been treated.[18] Nevertheless, Foucault argues that today's push for sexual identities and for environmental projects stems from a relatively recent socio-political impetus: the need to produce and manage life. This need developed in the late 18th century, with the very introduction of life as a tractable concept. When Cuvier founded biology, life replaced taxonomy as the salient mark of entities. "The living being now wraps itself in its own existence," Foucault explains, and is determined not by taxonomic locality but rather by its "conditions of life."[19] With Darwin's work

15. Take, for example, Corber and Valocchi, *Queer Studies: An Interdisciplinary Reader* (Oxford: Blackwell, 2006). See also Susan Stryker and Stephen Whittle (Editors), *The Transgender Studies Reader*, (New York: Routledge, 2006).

16. Lynne Huffer, *Mad for Foucault: Rethinking the Foundations of Queer Theory* (New York: Columbia University Press, 2010).

17. See, for instance, Eric Darier, *Discourses of the Environment*, (Malden: Blackwell, 1999), and the more recent Stephanie Rutherford, *Governing of the Wild: Ecotours of Power* (Minneapolis: University of Minnesota Press, 2011).

18. Michel Foucault, "The Ethics of the Concern for Self as Practice of Freedom," *Ethics, Subjectivity and Truth*, (New York: The New Press, 1994), 295. See also: Michel Foucault, *The History of Sexuality, Vol. 1: An Introduction*, (New York: Vintage, 1976).

19. Michel Foucault, *The Order of Things*, (New York: Vintage 1966), 274.

in the 19th century, those conditions of life began to signify conditions of the population.[20] Increasingly, society did not only treat human or other bodies as mere brute realities or even mechanistic capacities. It further saw human or other populations as centres of life-force, to be gripped and governed according to specifications relative to their species. Foucault terms this tactical turn 'biopower.'[21] It is as an object of biopower that both nature and sex become increasingly institutionalized. After all, the population must be controlled both externally and internally, through its milieu and its reproductive habits. It is no wonder, then, that sexual identity is so rampantly prompted and policed by the norms of heterosexual reproduction. And it is no wonder that much environmental activity relies upon the reproducibility of identifiable subjects, species, and systems. Both sexuality and nature are increasingly institutionalized throughout a biopolitical structure intent to produce and manage life.

Although quite suggestive, this is the extent of Foucault's direct contribution to ecological critique. His contribution to a critique of sexuality, however, goes much farther. In *The History of Sexuality*, for instance, Foucault takes sexuality as a target of biopower and places it within the context of power's institutionalization and resistance thereto. In several late interviews, Foucault further identifies human intimacy as a salient form of that resistance. Throughout his investigations, Foucault is interested in demonstrating not only that the institutionalization of sexuality involves the constitution of the subject through its confession to a sexual identity, but that resistance to this institutionalization demands the deconstruction of the subject through practices of physical intimacy. This deconstruction of the subject, I argue, lends a sense of strangeness to Foucault's intimacy that is reminiscent of Morton's account.

Consider first the constitution of the subject through its confession to identity, especial sexual identity. Today, Foucault muses, the educational, medical, and juridical realms demand that the subject speak. And, just as Christian confession proclaimed freedom but really constrained its participants, contemporary confession chains the subject to society's system of norms. The demand that a subject speak is a demand that it speak itself into subject-hood and thereby into a position of subjugation to the system determining subjects. Sexual confession is no exception. The question, 'what is my secret desire' directly corresponds to 'who am I.' Social media platforms and online surveys, for instance, typically prompt people to capture their identity by claiming a sex and a sexual orientation: usually male or female,

20. Michel Foucault, *Security, Territory, and Population* (New York: Palgrave, 1977-78), 78-79.
21. Foucault, *The History of Sexuality*, 147.

straight, gay, or bisexual. In claiming an identity, people acquiesce both to its prior construction and future use in the calculation of populations. For Foucault, 'I' am but a node in the nest of bureaucracy. The only way to disengage from the mores to which my sexual identity confines me is through the volatility of intimacy.

Foucault recommends intimate pleasure as a technique of resistance to the institutional subjugation enacted through confessional self subjectivation.[22] Pleasure, he writes, is "nothing other than an event, an event that happens, that happens, I would say, outside the subject, or at the limit of the subject, or between two subjects, in this something that is neither of the body nor of the soul, neither outside nor inside."[23] As such, it resists subjectivation on two levels. First, intimate pleasure disrupts self-identity. Pleasure, Foucault observes, is a transgressive, fragmented explosion. It reinstates the unsteady excesses of the body at the expense of self-unity. Second, intimate pleasure disrupts institutionalised identity. It creates affective alliances between people that subvert their categorical localities. Intimacy thereby fashions strands of excess in society which have the capacity to unhinge its mores.[24] "The intensities of pleasure," Foucault writes, "are linked to the fact that you de-subjugate yourself, that you cease to be a subject."[25] Through intimacy, 'I' find myself far from myself, having suddenly awoken to the strangeness of (not) being me. This is Foucault's call to deconstructive activity. It is a proposal of transformative intimacy.

Now, this call to intimacy, lying at the base of queer theory, has important implications for ecology and, ultimately, queer ecology. If queer intimacy strikes at the root of what makes sexual identity oppressive, and if environmental projects share the same root in a biopolitical regime, then intimacy must also upset environmental institutionalization and instigate a turn toward ecology. Sandilands argues precisely this point in "Sex at the Limits." Resistance to sexual regulation through non-normative intimacy, she states, is in fact tied to practicing transformative ecology.[26] In either case, intimacy necessarily includes estrangement. Just as Morton's mesh *requires* the strange stranger, so Foucault's pleasure *requires* the radical disruption of identity. I find myself an intimate stranger to myself and among intimate strangers.

---

22. Foucault, *The History of Sexuality*, 157.

23. Michel Foucault, "The Gay Science", *Critical Inquiry* 37.3 (2011), 389.

24. Michel Foucault, "Friendship as a Way of Life", in *Ethics: Subjectivity and Truth* (London: Penguin, 1998), 136 and 138.

25. Foucault, "The Gay Science", 399-400.

26. Catriona Sandilands, "Sex at the Limits," in *Discourses of the Environment*, Eric Darier (Editor), (Oxford: Blackwell, 1999), 91.

Queer Ecological Intimacy: A Poetics of Space / A Poetics of Spice

Morton's account of intimacy as requisite to ecological ethics and Foucault's account of intimacy as requisite to sexual ethics together suggest that intimacy is in fact a viable theoretical basis for something like queer ecology. Before culling a theory of intimacy here, it is helpful to review their accounts very schematically. Their conceptions of intimacy bear different emphases. Morton's account is heavily descriptive, whereas Foucault's is mildly prescriptive. But, more deeply, Morton focuses on intimacy between living and non-living entities, and therefore revels in its awkwardness, while Foucault focuses on intimacy between same-sex bodies, and therefore eulogizes its euphoric elements. Nevertheless, ultimately their accounts are commensurate. Not only does Morton acknowledge the desire and Foucault the milieu of intimacy, but, more importantly, both Morton and Foucault consider intimacy to be an experience of the limit in which beings and their boundaries are equally indistinguishable. For them, intimacy disrespects borders and detonates identities. Certainly, then, Morton is justified in asserting that ecology "demands intimacies with other beings that queer theory also demands, in another key."

Together, however, these accounts suggest something more than simply the viability of a composite term or even a discipline like 'queer ecology.' Consider them again in greater detail. On the one hand, Morton dispels the myth of Nature, at a distance from the subject, by pointing out the enmeshed or already intimate character of existence. As an implication of this existence, Morton then notes a disillusionment with Nature and an estrangement among things. On the other hand, Foucault dispels the myth of the subject, at a distance from Nature, by pointing out its already constructed character and calling for a deconstructive intimacy. As a reverberation of this deconstructive intimacy, moreover, Foucault observes a certain disillusionment with systems of subjectivation and an estrangement from oneself. Collectively, then, both Morton and Foucault counter a false distance between subject and object with a commendation to intimacy; and both consequently suppose that intimacy inaugurates disillusionment and estrangement. But what is disillusionment and what is estrangement if it is not some form of distance? I therefore argue that Morton and Foucault counter distance with intimacy only to get more distance ~ a different distance. The distance they dispel is false and impersonal, whereas the distance they inaugurate is not. What this essay affords, then, is not merely a confirmation of the term 'queer ecology' but a definition of intimacy. *This* is intimacy: the transmutation of distance ~ a transmutation from illusory distance to a distance of disillusionment ~ or, again, from a distance between strangers to an estranged distance.

In order to elucidate my proposal that intimacy is the transmutation of distance, I turn to Gaston Bachelard. Bachelard, an important inspiration for both Morton and Foucault,[27] concerned himself directly with the question of intimacy in space. In his book *The Poetics of Space*, he analyses different images of intimate space, one of which is perhaps the intimate space *par excellence*: the home. One might think that the home protects me from the outside, serving as a cocoon to keep the world at bay, but Bachelard suggests this is a gross oversimplification. The home, he insists, is never just a home; it is always not itself, not exactly itself, not quite itself. Every home opens out to the universe and onto the very world from which it supposedly keeps one safe. "In this dynamic rivalry between house and universe," Bachelard writes, "inhabited space transcends geometrical space;" "a house that has been experienced is not an inert box."[28] He then goes on to consider the home as a 'spiral,' a 'surface,' a 'threshold' which of necessity creates a vortex between insides and outsides.

The home's intimate character has as much to do with its closures as its openings. The home is familiar and it is uncanny; it is a place of rest and a space for awful reverie. As such, the home demonstrates that intimacy does not mean privacy or self-same unity, but rather signifies a rearrangement of geographical space in phenomenological space. In this way, Bachelard not only confirms my proposal that intimacy is the transmutation of distance but contributes the illustrative metaphor of a spiral.

In closing, let me draw just one implication from the preceding argument. Recall that Morton asserts, following his defence of intimacy as equally important for ecology and queer theory, that "fully and properly, ecology *is* queer theory and queer theory *is* ecology: queer ecology."[29] I have already remarked that this emphasis on the 'is' over the 'is not' privileges the mesh over the strange stranger, identification over disidentification. Indeed, by collapsing these disciplines into one another, Morton enervates the revolutionary character of his intimate proposal. If intimate things just *are* one another, we risk devolving into tautological nonsense. But Morton is astute to suspect that the significance of intimacy bears dramatic implications not just for subjects and objects, queer theory and ecology, but even more broadly for the nature of interdisciplinarity. Having argued that intimacy is the transmutation of distance, I suggest that intimacy between disciplines must mean at least two

---

27. See Timothy Morton *Poetics of Spice: Romantic Consumerism and the Exotic,* (Cambridge: Cambridge University Press, 2006), and Foucault's "Interview with Michel Foucault," *Power (The Essential Works of Foucault, 1954-1984),* by Michel Foucault, James D. Faubion, and Robert Hurley, (New York: New Press, 2001).

28. Gaston Bachelard, *The Poetics of Space* (Boston: Beacon Press, 1958), 47, 225.

29. Gaston Bachelard, *The Poetics of Space,* Ibid.

things. First, neither discipline is wholly distinct or set at a distance from the other. Second, neither discipline is wholly indistinct, or made to dissolve into the other. Instead, both are awkwardly porous entities. Ideally, interdisciplinary research makes disciplines intimate with one another not by claiming that they are each other but rather by drawing them together to such a degree that each might be disenchanted and estranged. Interdisciplinarity, then, will function in a spiralling manner, producing ever greater alignment as well as distinctive clarity.

In this essay, I have proposed that intimacy, defined as the transmutation of distance, is not only a theoretical element of queer theory and ecology, respectively, but also a necessary condition of queer ecology. I have further taken this intimacy to be, in the case of queer ecology, both transformative and resistant to institutionalization. I do not claim that intimacy is a sufficient condition for queer ecology. I do, however, trust that a robust definition of intimacy is an important contribution along the way.

Perry Zurn

She-Wolf:

I Want (to be Come on (to))) the (she)-wolf, or, How Many Aphorisms Does it Take to Reverse Platonism?[1]

Abstract: In his Plato or Paul: The Origins of Western Homophobia, *Theodore W. Jennings reveals the late Plato's Laws as a set of homophobic texts, in contrast to earlier writings, such as the Phaedrus, that celebrate man's love of boys as a philosophical means of attaining to the ideal of Beauty. Both the lover / beloved structure of this love, and Plato's late exiling of same-sex sex from the ideal state (as went the poet before it), leaves queer sex in a pickle. My project asks three questions, prompted by Jennings' careful scholarship: first, how might queer erotic practices transform the lover / beloved relationship; second, how might one wrest the capital "B" from "Beauty" to cultivate philosophical-erotic work and play that transforms singularities, eradicating the alienating and homogenizing Ideal; and third, what precisely are we doing when we philosophize and perform practices that the Laws suggests are "unthinkable"?*

"As wolves love lambs so lovers love their beloveds." ~ Plato, Phaedrus.

If hierarchical love is an old effect of grammar, and the distinction between lover and beloved potentially undecidable, how lone of a she-wolf am I? Once one destabilizes the distinction, is there indeed, as Menexenus mockingly suggests, no friend (in love) at all? Further, in the philosophical-sexual movement toward beauty, if I must leave behind each beloved or be left behind by each lover once mine, how greatly does my loneliness increase in proportion to my philosophical venture? Plato would have me dropping or dropped love like flies to grow the plumage necessary to achieve the Ideal; I want to taste and watch die the feathers in each of my beddings, as Barbara Johnson translates Derrida's pun on to seed and to fuck in "Plato's Pharmacy."

In the interstices of the Platonic homophobic turn that Jennings articulates, queer sex, or to put it slightly differently, Foucault's "bodies and pleasures," disorganizes, rebecomes, twisting to fit its gradual eviction from human society. The subject of this sex(uality or ~ ies) is rendered increasingly animal to the point, almost, of inexpressability: even in (dubious) companioned ascent toward the Ideal, lover and beloved "share" the same plumage *because* of their love; the more hierarchical view renders the lover a wolf seducing a lamb. What Jill Johnston calls "lesbian chauvinism," what Virgil W. Brower might call a kind of "wolfishness," is at best undecidable in Plato's renderings of same-sex sexing. Given the impossibility of sexual equality in his *Laws*, O wolf, O rap-tor who seizes me, what becomes of your beastialized identity when I, in turn, seize you?

lato
rotic hierarchy
ueer
ingularity
nthinkable
ennings
he philosophic-erotic

If you hang me from your ceiling; if you beat long leaving heaving lashes into the curve of my back until I scream: I seek, O anonymous Athenian, I seek a certain rap-tor. I am a lovely shepherd boy; I'll tell you my Greek *nom de plume* if through this rape, this rap-ture, O my raptor, we can wrest Beauty down from the sky in a double-reversal of Platonism:

First, rather than swimming in Diotima's absolute "sea of beauty," we must lap it up, opposing the cult of generality until we arrive at the particular; scratch that, the singular; scratch that, what I mean to say is that I want each scratch of the wolf at my back as I come to fucking count as immanently beautiful. This time around reversing Platonism means that every strike across my ass undoes the "process of abstraction from the imperious and… inconvenient insistence of the body" (Jennings).

Second: The inculcation of "common fame" prescribed in the *Laws* renders anything other than the same-sex taboo "unthinkable," making sex and philosophy, making queer philosophy a secret, a practice of secrets in a closet. Plato's homogeneous prescription for society exiles the "what if it were otherwise" of our illustrious keynote (Golding); exiles to the unthinkable his, or his Socrates' own fuck-until-you-sweat-philosophy scenario.

Without this, I am alone. In the wake of fuck-philosophy, the only practice left for me? To sex that unthinkable with which he formed society. The only remaining practice for a she-wolf stripped of bedding-beauty is to fuck the law(s) themselves until she wrings water from stone.

Sarah Mann O'Donnell

1. A response to Theodore W. Jennings' *Plato or Paul: The Origins of Western Homophobia* (Cleveland, The Pilgrim Press, 2009). Presented in the roundtable "The Platonic Invention of the Closet," in collaboration with the Paul of Tarsus Working Interdisciplinary Group, at *Queer(ing) Poetics: Text, Method, Movement, Thought*, Chicago, Northwestern University's 2011 Queertopia! Conference.

Jennuflectings II:

Outing Plato with the Salt & Savour of Rome

Taken from the text, Brower writes: The crux of Jenning's argument is his reading of Plato's Laws, showing how the tolerance of same-sex relations in the earlier Platonic dialogues is called into question, if not utterly condemned and rejected in this, one of his later ones. Jennings offers insightful historical and political motivations as to why this Platonic anomaly may have come about. If you think you know your Plato (or would like to) and have swallowed the standard talking-points served up by so many university-level Introduction to Philosophy classes (including some of my own) about how open and friendly Platonic philosophy is to homosexuality (if such a word can be used here) or homophilia (for lack of a better word), then the first 50 pages of Jenning's book is a must-read. You must read it, like: tonight. The image of the de facto gay-friendly Plato is all the more dangerous because it is so tacitly presupposed ~ so uncritically accepted ~ that it seems almost genetically to pass down through the educated classes. And at the very least, regardless of the Christian apologetics he seems at times to slip into for better or worse, Jennings' text is a remarkable success insofar as he makes a very strong case in very few pages, rendering accessible to a wide audience (at least those with ears to hear) all the tools necessary to overcome this crippling naïveté. To out Plato: he, who very well may have invented the closet, as, himself, a closet-homophobe is utterly scandalous and utterly necessary and for that Ted [Jennings] deserves our attention and applause.

> In the case of *attentat sans violence*, the offense in which the police have been unable to find anything, nothing at all, in that case the criminal is simply a criminal because he is criminal, because he has those tastes.
> ~ Guy Hocquenghem[1]

> But Christianity can also be so lenient or flavoured with sweetness that all the attempts to perk up the appetite and give people a taste for it...are futile and end up making people disgusted with it. No, there must be salt in the food. And the New Testament really takes care of that...No, the appetite has to be aroused in a different way.
> ~ Søren Kierkegaard[2]

1. Guy Hocquenghem, "The Danger of Child Sexuality," trans Alan Sheridan in *Foucault Live: Collected Interviews*, 1961-1984, (New York: Semiotext(e), 1989), 268.
2. Søren Kierkegaard, "Judge for Yourself! For Self-Examination Recommended to the Present Age" in *Kierkegaard's Writings*, Vol. XXI *For Self-Examination / Judge For Yourself!*, trans Howard V. Hong and Edna H. Hong. Hong, (New Jersey: Princeton University Press, 1990), 203.

I relish my reading of this text, *Plato or Paul?: The Origins of Western Homophobia,*[3] which I believe deserves to be placed alongside Peter Brown's *The Body and Society* as a dangerous supplement to *The History of Sexuality* project set in motion by Michel Foucault. It is a genealogy of morals in every sense. (Or, maybe more so in one specific sense than the other senses.) It is difficult to respond critically ~ or remain truly critical in one's response ~ to a book with which one is in so much agreement; a sentiment I have experienced than once when engaging a text by Ted Jennings. So what follows is often more response than criticism; detours, in the Heideggerian sense. As Heidegger says when responding to Hölderlin, what follows are merely remarks; trying to attend-to a text worth attending-to. One of the most useful things you learn in seminary is to criticize those you adore. Criticism is the only way to take someone seriously. And if at times I bear my teeth, or even bite, it is with the same mouth that kisses.

In one of Hélène Cixous recent novels, entitled Philippines, one finds a discussion between mother and daughter in which the-writer-that-Cixous-is discloses the taste of the letter and remarks how letters, themselves, have a taste:

> I rang up my daughter straightaway. I wanted to share this with her...
>
> ~ Philippine, I said, do you know what it is?
> ~ Philippine? No, I don't. Do *you* know? ...Is it something obscene? she suggested.
>
> I laughed. She laughed. Something obscene? Who knows?
> Then I said:
> ~ The almond. It's the almond. (I meant to say: it's the almond's lover [*amant*] perhaps).
> ~ It's an almond? How could I know this? Oh! it's an *amande* written with an *e*...
> ~ If you write it with an *a*, you'll enjoy its taste.

Rewriting a word with the letter *a*, of course, invokes Jacques Derrida's respelling of difference. The aftertaste or foretaste of *differance* lingers about the taste of the letter a, which, itself, renders the word or name of an almond more enjoyable; an almond, which already has an ambiguous taste (both bitter

3. Jennings, T. W. *Plato or Paul?: The Origins of Western Homophobia*, (Cleveland, The Pilgrim Press, 2009).

and sweet; both male and female; the very fruit of Cixousian bisexuality: a hard and bitter seminal seed with an inner milky maternal sweetness). This has something to do with the taste of a lover; specifically a French kind of lover; amant. And let's not lose track of this taste of letters and lovers shared between mother and daughter as we encounter Jennings' reading of a certain Roman love letter about the relation between man and boy; which is to say between father and son; god and Jesus. (We would do well to add a few more women, mothers, and daughters to Jennings' treatise, when we can.)

As Jennings investigates the genealogy of homophobia, he displays certain sapience for the taste of love and letters. It is on an anonymous letter addressed to Diognetes (that is even speculated to be a pseudonym of the Roman emperor, Hadrian) that Jennings writes of a kind of savouring. The intent of the letter in question, written sometime in the second century of the common era, is "to persuade the reader that Christianity, far from being a threat to the public weal of the empire, is the *very salt and savor* of that empire." Jennings' reading is that the writer of the Diognetes letter finds a kind of Christianity to be the salt and savour of Rome. Jennings then emphasizes certain sections of the letter to illuminate this thing called "Christianity" at its most salty and savoury.

(While I'm on the subject, I must say that I find this particular text of Jennings to be his most blatant apologetic for what Nietzsche calls "that stroke of genius called Christianity." In other texts and on other occasions, the salt and savor of Ted Jennings comes across not so much as Christianity, proper, but rather more palatable entities, such as the gospel, or the Pauline tradition; the kind of entities that one can find defended by folks as diverse, atheistic, and irreligious as Heidegger, Badiou, Lacan, Freud, Kristeva, Derrida, or Engels. The overarching thesis of Jennings text is that homophobia is not so much Christian as Greek. It is the result of the bastardization of Paul or the gospel through the legacy of Hellenization that is apostate from their true textual tradition. Does this thing called Christianity deserve to be so defended? The very structure, title, and architectonic of the Jenning's argument is not so much that homophobia isn't Christian but that it isn't Pauline; isn't true to more than a very few scant references throughout the whole of the Hebrew Bible, nor the gospel of Matthew. But that's what "Christianity" is, isn't it?: nothing but the mutation of the gospel and Pauline theory by Greco-Latin thinkers and ideas.)

But back to the letter to Diognetes. The letter reads: "What the soul is to the body, Christians are to the world." The god of such a world-soul acts "as one who saves by persuasion, not compulsion, for compulsion is no attribute of God." What comes about is a relation between saving and savouring; between the soteriology of Diognetes and the tongue of Jennings. The salt of Ted Jennings is the savour of a kind of Christianity; one which seems to taste more savoury than sweet; more seminal than milky.

It would be the taste of a love tradition that savours beloveds; one which does so by way of persuasion rather than compulsion. One of the key issues in Jennings' text is to show the crucial difference between pederasty and paedophilia; the former as a practice of persuasion, seduction, or consent, the latter as one of nonconsensual predation upon pre-pubescent children. This all tarries upon the concept of, "the corruption of youths" or "*paidophthoria*," in Greek. Jennings goes to great pains to show the perhaps flippant translation of paidophthoria as "pederasty" and how such a tactical mistranslation plays no small role in the instauration of a kind of double-edged ageism, the demonisation of consensual post-pubescent same-sex relations, and even its conflation into a rejection of same-sex relations, on the whole. One of the many tasty morsels in Jenning's text is his disclosing of the culprits who try to sneak or smuggle paidophthoria, corrupting the youth (the very allegation levelled against Socrates), or perhaps what would best be translated as paedophilia (a breed of non-consensual pre-pubescent child abuse) into the Ten Commandments. The smugglers are Clement of Alexandria, Barnabas, and the *Didache* (the teaching of the twelve disciples). "Of course in no known version of the Bible does such a commandment anywhere appear."[4] Leave that to Leviticus.

The crux of Jenning's argument is his reading of Plato's Laws, showing how the tolerance of same-sex relations in the earlier Platonic dialogues is called into question, if not utterly condemned and rejected in this, one of his later ones. Jennings offers insightful historical and political motivations as to why this Platonic anomaly may have come about (e.g., Sparta's overtaking of Athens and the need for less passive Athenian citizens). If you think you know your Plato (or would like to) and have swallowed the standard talking-points served up by so many university-level Introduction to Philosophy classes (including some of my own) about how open and friendly Platonic philosophy is to homosexuality (if such a word can be used here) or homophilia (for lack of a better word), then the first 50 pages of Jenning's book is a must-read. You must read it, like: tonight. The image of the de facto gay-friendly Plato is all the more dangerous because it is so tacitly presupposed ~ so uncritically accepted ~ that it seems almost *genetically* to pass down through the educated classes. And at the very least, regardless of the Christian apologetics he seems at times to slip into for better or worse, Jennings' text is a remarkable success insofar as he makes a very strong case in very few pages, rendering accessible to a wide audience (at least those with ears to hear) all the tools necessary to overcome this crippling naïveté. To out Plato: he, who very

4. Jennings, *Plato or Paul ?*, 162.

well may have invented of the closet,[5] as, himself, a closet-homophobe is utterly scandalous and utterly necessary and for that Ted deserves our attention and applause.

If we agree with Jennings argument, which I am inclined to do, the story doesn't stop with Plato but would stretch further back to the gender roles which Plato and the Hellenics made use of to condemn same-sex relations. After Jennings analysis, the origins (if there are such things) of Western homophobia seem to be sexism; or at least different androcentrisms or caricatures of womanhood present in both the Greek and Hebrew traditions that either render passivity shameful and a sexual woman as only ever passive, or nature as the fetish of procreation rendering women as mere baby-making machines. Jennings, of course, understands this and speaks of it. But the point would be that the arche-homophobe, be it Plato or the writer of Leviticus, is always already dependent on the gender stereotypes which they in turn can use or abuse.

And it must never be forgotten (and I'm not suggesting that Jennings has forgotten this) that it is not so much that Plato is the homophobe but rather the anonymous "Athenian" in Plato's *Laws*. Derridean that he is, Jennings knows better than most how gifted, clever, and complicated a writer Plato is. Jennings seems to suffer a certain Clementine disease. Just as Clement of Alexandria ~ in his textual engagement with the gospel ~ had to acquiesce that Jesus wasn't married, but still tries to make the case that Paul also was married (a untenable claim!), Jennings ~ in his careful and responsible textual engagement with the *Laws* ~ also has to acquiesce that it is the Athenian who is homophobic, yet he still makes the case that Plato also was homophobic. *Ecce homo*: Jennings of Alexandria! Is he trapped in an unjust synecdochal machine? If not a blatant logical fallacy of composition, confusing a part of Plato with the whole of Plato? Is it merely because it would sell fewer copies that this text is not entitled, *The Anonymous Athenian or Paul?* But I should not be unfair.

At times Jennings does talk of homophobia as a "position that Plato...put in the mouth of the Athenian."[6] Jennings takes great pleasure in putting things in and pulling things out of the mouths of others. It is one of his tropes that one can trace back as early as his 1988 text called *Liturgy of Liberation* in which he endeavours to take the act of forgiveness out of the mouths of priests.

But as fabulous as Jennings' reading of Plato is I'm more struck by his reading of Xenophon's version of the *Symposium*, specifically the importance of the kiss. Xenophon's Socrates addresses the erotic expressions of the same-sex couple, Clinias and Critobulus, by stating that the latter has even

5. Jennings, *Plato or Paul ?*, 50.
6. Jennings, *Plato or Paul?*, 56.

kissed Clinias, and nothing is a fiercer *inducement to* love than that. It's an insatiable thing, and it produces a kind of *delicious anticipation*. That's why I say that anyone who wants to be able to behave *responsibly* ought to refrain from kissing the young and attractive." Jennings follows his quotation with his own question: "Is this to be taken ironically, or does it presage something more critical?"[7] I'd like to invite him, today, to say more about the answer to this question, if he has one. I was not quite sure if the possible presaging of something more critical comes three pages later when he mentions that another of Xenophon's characters kisses one of the dancing girls at the symposium and that this may be a kind of "reprogramming of same-sex love into heterosexual desire."[8] That's crucial enough.

Perhaps it is because consummation of same-sex love is to become so shameful in Xenophon that any inducement to consummation by kissing is what makes it so crucial since Jennings' discussion moves to the shamefulness of gratifying sexual desires which should remain in anticipation. If you don't kiss, then the love is not delicious enough to act further on; something found in Phaedrus' account of Achilles and Patroclus in Plato's Symposium as though "they were lovers, but they didn't have sex."[9] Jennings calls this, for good reason, "hermeneutical bravado." And if such hermeneutical bravado assumes that Achilles and Patroclus did not have sex because they did not kiss, it renders all the more striking how Kleist has Achilles be kissed to death (so to speak) not by a same-sex partner, but by a woman, Penthesilea, Queen of the Amazons. The kiss is delicious anticipation, but it is delicious. As such, kissing annuls responsibility in that it induces one to love; to love further than mere kissing. If only kissing could take the place of sexual love. As Freud says, "It's a shame I can't kiss myself." One can only miss such kisses. But if consummation is being used to shame same-sex desire, then resistance to such shame-mongering would endeavour above all things to kiss often and to kiss hard.

If it is the delicious aspect of kissing that moves honourable anticipation into shameful consummation, then perhaps one should kiss less delicious parts; kissing something more bitter than sweet; or, better, perhaps placing a dollop of the sweet and delicious on (or in) what are alleged to be the bitterest of places. Such possibilities lead us to Jennings' quick mention of the Roman repugnance of oral sex, which seems to have everything to do with the unnaturalness of sexuality not aimed at procreation; what Plato referred to as "its wasting of the seed of life on a stony and rocky soil" and what will come to

---

7. Jennings, *Plato or Paul?*, 53.
8. Jennings, *Plato or Paul?*, 56.
9. Jennings, *Plato or Paul?*, 55.

be, much later, what Philo condemns as sowing seeds "in ponds or mountain streams instead of the plains," which he considers one does when having sex with a menstruating woman. We should not overlook that, as such, oral sex can serve as both a hetero- and homosexual rebellion against the very tools of homophobia. Perhaps the strongest stance an ally can take in solidarity with lgbtq+ friends is with the tongue. Licking, kissing, sucking, and all forms of the '-linguses' of oral sexualities would become efficacious political resistances to vanilla intolerances. (Not that vanilla can't be delicious.)

The Encratite were an early Christian group that forbade all kinds of sexual intercourse; for example, Tatian (who may have been a student of Justin Martyr). For the Encratite, pederasty, adultery, and sex, in general, are all deplorable. But I do not think it responsible (perhaps Jennings has suffered too many kisses) to say, as he does about Tatian, that "it was not a problem to class marriage along with adultery and the corruption (or rape) of youths, since *it was all the same for him*."[10] Converse accident: Just because the celibates may be forced to look down on all forms of sexual intercourse, it does not necessarily follow that they think, by consequence, that rape and consensual sex are "all the same."

Jennings addresses the Roman dread of oral sex twice. First, it follows one of Seutonius' account of Tiberius, who is alleged to have trained "little boys, whom he called his 'minnows,' to...get between his legs [while he was swimming] to lick and nibble him."[11] This implicates Tiberius in both paedophilia and the unnaturalness of oral sex, making oral sex guilty by association; a tactic used throughout Jennings' genealogy of homophobia that often uses guilt by association as a red herring to condemn same-sex practices by suggesting their proximity to bestiality, incest, (or even murder and genocide, in Plato). On this point, at times when Jennings highlights such a mismatch with incest his insistence on the mismatch seems a tacit assent with the mismatches that incest *must* be wrong; something I would not necessarily expect from him and that I don't think should go without saying. Wouldn't such an agreement and allowance of the de facto condemnation of incest (by which I mean post-pubescent and consensual sex between consanguineous relations) be just as deplorable as the de facto condemnation of same-sex eroticism?

The second address to Roman oral sex has to do with the emperor, Nero. Suetonius reports that "Nero practiced every kind of obscenity, and after defiling almost every part of his body finally invented a novel game: he

10. Jennings, *Plato or Paul?*, 164.
11. Jennings, *Plato or Paul?*, 149.

was released from a cage dressed in the skins of wild animals, and attacked the private parts of men and women who stood bound to stakes."[12] Jennings comments that "Nero has outraged Roman sensibilities by finding a way to combine oral sex (repugnant to the Romans) with rape and torture (and execution). This is novelty by which Nero completes the work of 'defiling every part of his body.'"[13]

Oh, iterability! Four lines after just quoting Suetonius, Jennings misquotes that very quote and paints Nero in even a worse light than Suetonius had.

Again, Suetonius: "defiling almost every part of his body."

Jennings quoting Suetonius: "defiling every part of his body."

Almost, Ted. It's a Pauline disease, I suppose, to alter a citation after one cites it. Or maybe it's a Matthew syndrome, who when quoting Isaiah changes the word "servant" to "lad" or "boy" [*pais*].[14] Nero is not said to defile every part of his body but to *almost* defile every part of his body. After writing so much about smugglers, Jennings can't resist becoming one. At least Jenning smuggles out rather than smuggles in, but, Jesus, why not smuggle a commandment or two out of the Decalogue.

In no way do I wish to defend Nero, but rather to show how Jennings, himself, is not immune to what he alleges against Phaedrus, earlier, as "hermeneutic bravado." It should not go without saying that Nero is combining oral sex with anything at all. Nero could sew his mouth shut and would still be able to attack "the private parts of men and women" if only with his hands and penis. Of course it could be a description of oral sex, but it doesn't necessarily have to be. I make this observation on two points. First, I think my reading of Suetonius, here, is indicative of the kind of apologetic hermeneutics Ted makes when trying to offer alternative readings of someone like Paul (e.g. on nature). Secondly, that even in Nero ~ the most obscene of the obscene ~ Suetonius yet gives us hope that not all parts of the body are defiled. In those of us who defile *almost* every part of our body, there is perhaps one part that resists and that part of the body, I would suggest, could be the tongue. The point is not that the tongue is beyond defilement, but rather that it can accomplish things, in a very singular way, that no other sense-organ or appendage can. It renders the mouth neither simply an orifice, nor itself as simply an appendage. The tongue can play the game of penetration and at the same time refuse to penetrate. It can be inside or outside. It discloses that the inside is the outside. It can lick and nibble on the surface or stretch

---

12. Jennings, *Plato or Paul?*, 151-2.
13. Jennings, *Plato or Paul?* Ibid.
14. Jennings, *Plato or Paul?*, 171.

and strain to the depths. The tongue is the surface, itself. That stroke of genius called the salt and savour of Rome by Jennings, as well as that saltiness Kierkegaard discerns and encourages others to savour in a Christianity-to-come (which, thereby, arouses or seduces in different ways) cannot be relished without "the salt and savour" of Ted Jennings.

Virgil Bower

Designing Atonal Rhythms

Abstract: Design is the paradigmatic space of encounter between form and function, rationality and sensuality, objectivity and subjectivity. To design a book or a journal which includes text and image, without privileging one over the other, or without relinquishing any of those concerns requires an especially subtle choreography between all these attributes, in addition to re-staging research as an expression of risk. One could say every design is 'an event', one which allows each aspect to play its part and for each to be acknowledged and seen as important. As the chains of equivalence and points of divergence between and amongst these aspects is not always exposed or evident, these remarks are intended as an exposé of the process and decisions undertaken in the course of the design at hand. This is especially important when working on a brief as complex as that of Zētēsis, which, by its very conceptualisation and content, intends to expose the cruelty of the classical canon.[1]

"Language is the material of sense." ~ Hannah Lammin.[2]

With and Against the Canon

The designer and typographer are always mediating the ~ sometimes conflictual ~ attributes noted above, while at the same time attempting to negotiate between the needs and desires of readers; researchers and a highly regarded academic publishing house, whose concerns are for clarity of communication, rigour and solid evidence of research, all of which can and should be expressed in and by the design.

Canons are comforting. They refer to well trodden paths and known entities. In any field of inquiry, canons of knowledge become the dominant force in any encounter we may have with the work before us: they are the memories we don't even realise we have, drawing us inexorably towards the known ground of our intellectual and aesthetic endeavours. They enframe us, even as we attempt to depart from them. They are inevitable. Even welcome, since without something to break away from, we have no ground from which to depart; no limit to transgress.

1. The classical canons of design are many; they include the Golden Section (Phi, 1.86), which forms the basis of the 'canons of page construction' for books, from the Medieval period. 'There was a time when deviations from the truly beautiful page proportions 2:3, $1:\sqrt{3}$, and the Golden Section were rare. Many books produced between 1550 and 1770 show these proportions exactly, to within half a millimeter'. Jan Tschichold, *The Form of the Book*, (Hartley & Marks, 1991). The Western canon is the dominant literary force, shaping cultural and intellectual priorities, and design is an ally to the dissemination of such a canon through its role in typography and book design.

2. Hannah Lammin in conversation with Sheena Calvert, 12th September 2013.

anonical
tonal
na-fractious
recarious
rystal goblet
ogue
ischief
ythm

"By all means break the rules, and break them beautifully, deliberately and well."[3] ~ Robert Bringhurst, *The Elements of Typographic Style.*

As Robert Bringhurst suggests, these concerns are especially true of typography ~ an art which is both scientific and poetic. It embraces and exemplifies the dualities of exactitude and expression, subjectivity and objectivity, respect for rules, and risk. Whilst reaching for the elusive goal of transparency ~ for the 'window' which Beatrice Warde and other typographic purists have coveted ~ typography is always already a form of mediation: it exists as a physical interface between ourselves and meaning, and in doing so it plays a part in constructing that meaning.[4] However, even a crystal clear window has a presence, albeit a subtle one. Without material text[s] on paper, or screen, the event of written language; its performativity, its presence, would not exist and the force of these thoughts would remain mute. In its role as the concrete form of language, typography is the constant reminder that meaning is made, not pre-given: it 'matters', in every sense and nuance of that statement; its materiality is a fact, and a partner in the experience of reading. Typography is also a micro and macro art. To see the whole performance across a series of pages, as an event of reading, is as important as being aware of the details of an em-dash, chosen for its slightly queer curvature, or the slight deviations from the canon which Goudy ~ the typeface used here ~ implies; with its enchanted oddities, graceful and misbehaving.

There are parallels with philosophy, wherein the overall argument needs to be seen in relation to the details of linguistic expression and rhetorical phraseology. The very form[s] of language become the texture of the argument, just as the typeface forms the texture of the page. Philosophy and its manifestation through typography and design are intimately entwined, and need to be brought into constant relation as a seamless presentation of form and content ~ even where even visual dissonance is the counterpart to philosophical argument. These are subtle questions, and ones that are not so evident to the untrained eye. However, the typeface chosen for Zētēsis, and the subtleties of typographic detail are not accidental, nor are they arbitrary. They attempt to pay homage to the richness and detail of philosophical exposition in all its forms, and to actively work with, and not against, those

---

3. Robert Bringhurst, *The Elements of Typographic Style,* (Hartley & Marks, Canada, 4th edition, 2012), 10.

4. Beatrice Warde, *The Crystal Goblet*, (London: Sylvan Press, 1955). We refer here to Beatrice Warde's essay on typography "The Crystal Goblet", which was first delivered as a talk entitled "Printing Should be Invisible", first given to the British Typographer's Guild at the St. Bride Institute in London, October 7th, 1930. The essay's title refers to the clearest vessel of wine as a metaphor for the role of the printed word as providing no obstruction to the presentation of content.

myriad expressions of conceptual content, while being a 'window' which is acknowledged as both crystal clear and fully present.

We opened these remarks by claiming that there is no full objectivity in any design, but only a series of subjective choices that make the human presence felt. Design is a *human* activity, full of ambiguities, inflections, and contradictions, wherein technology is only ever a means, and the allure of its deterministic rationality is but a chimera. Subjectivity makes design an especially demanding encounter and negotiation between the reader and the author; one in which the designers' hand is always present as a third party, or a silent interlocutor. With this in mind, within this design we have tried to navigate these poles and the differing requirements of the present context, with a steady hand, a human eye for detail, and the potential for gently critiquing the canon while acknowledging its persistent force and presence, and its defining role.

This is how we resolved the brief given to us by a journal whose unusual remit for presenting the intersecting landscapes of art, philosophy and science privileges research generated by curiosity. First, we removed the images from the main part of the journal and set them into a separate insert as a remark on the ways in which artwork and text, the discursive and the figural, both diverge and differ between themselves while at the same exact time create dialogue and 'make' sense (differently).[5] These artworks, seen as a group, with their associated texts, are tangentially linked, through something akin to the philosophical aesthetic of Deleuze's *Logic of Sense*, one where the narrative is about difference, not identity, and about the non-equivalent in place of a sequential narrative.[6] The images play differently in this space, and take up Paul Klee's call not to reproduce what we can already see, but to make visible what we cannot. Deleuze states this as 'rendering visible forces that are not themselves visible,'[7] which shares the aim of philosophy to ask 'How can we see what we did not see before'?[8]

In the drawing together of images and artworks which support the philosophical departure points presumed by those questions, we posed another series of interrelated questions, which made sense in terms of the subversive and sensual forces of art, and the different logic they offer. Stated differently, this paper-bound 'gallery' of images operates as a space of visual reading which

5. On this point, see the important work by Jean-Françoise Lyotard, *Discourse, Figure,* trans Antony Hudek and Mary Lydon, (Minnesota: University of Minnesota Press, 2011).

6. Giles Deleuze, *The Logic of Sense*, introduction by Constantin Boundas, trans Mark Lester and Charles Stivale, (New York: Columbia University Press, 1990).

7. Deleuze Gilles, *Francis Bacon: The Logic of Sensation,* trans Daniel W. Smith, (London: Continuum, 2003).

8. Ibid.

invites a mediation on the ways in which images might randomly interact with one another, in contrast to their role as support or illustrations for texts. In being given an autonomous space, their treatment subverts the usual hierarchy of text versus image, in which text frequently wins out as the dominant discursive vehicles by which knowledge is disseminated. This creates a space for images to have an equivalent role in the communication of knowledge, and in posing a critique of how knowledge is formed per the canon, especially within the canonical object called the 'book.'

We therefore invite you to "see" or "read" (or "listen to") these images as forming a body of questions, not as supporting the texts within the journal, or operating as visual equivalents for philosophical ideas. The artworks possess their own dynamic force-field; one related, but not secondary, to the textual content which either accompanies them in short form, or to that of the journal. Image and text are not to be seen as being in opposition, but as possessing / performing their own discreet mode[s] of communication, and it was this premise that underpinned our desire both to amplify and question the ways in which these modes take place. Finally, and to borrow a term from Thomas Hirshorn made in reference to the *Gramsci Memorial*, we wanted them to form 'precarious moments of grace,'[9] moments in which they possess a presence of their own.

We wished to enact a sub-textual intervention into questions of the canon, via the subtleties of punctuation rendered slightly strange, in the form of stray commas or wave-line em-dashes. Punctuation is a clear instance where material language affects the establishment of meaning in language. There are two kinds of punctuation, one that is rhetorical and based on pauses and breath (voiced); the other that is grammatical and related to the interactions of parts of speech (silent). Such conventions as capitalization, paragraph spacing and indents of course also count as punctuation, since they order the flow of ideas in a text. Initially, the function for which punctuation was created was purely rhetorical: it aided the classical reader in knowing when to pause and where to place accents and inflections of voice when reading aloud from a text. It has become a mark of the performative in language, the vocal / acoustic, and the choreographic. This repertoire of marks, developed and added to over time, has become codified and regularised part of written language similarly moving, as did language, from the oral world into the silent, written world, later reinforcing grammatical roles, not just temporal ones. In contemporary times, the syntactical role of punctuation has entered yet another phase, the result

9. See Thomas Hirschhorn's, *Gramsci Monument*, in the Forest Houses; the Bronx. Through the artist being present, and producing something (in this case, public art), Hirschhorn seeks to create such 'precarious moments of grace' from the temporary alignment of the produced and the observer, who needs to be both present and 'awake' to the potential of the work.

of the standardization and control of language made possible (and politically deemed necessary) by the new technology of printing. This shift has profoundly affected thought and reorganized our relationship to language (and language to itself) in ways which have deep implications for knowledge gained through the written form, and for the canonical object we call 'the book': that sequence of pages which are punctuated by the rhythms of material language in familiar and standardized ways; in turn regulating meaning and its association with the establishment of truth.

In Zētēsis, by disrupting the strictly linear 'movement' of language, through turned letters and strange punctuation, we sought to disrupt its ordinary rhythms, and to perform a different 'movement': one which is closer to the non-structures of improvisation than conventional musical form. We have therefore, by analogy, 'punctuated' the typographic and compositional rhythms of this book, differently, with a view to exposing and complementing the atonal and non-conventional forms of thought presented here, in a move which constitutes both an acceptance of the necessity of the canon, and at the same time, its refusal. Zētēsis celebrates the paradoxical, a-logical, sensual characteristics of language, freed from the necessities of instrumentality, by 'playing' it slightly differently. We have therefore included within these pages some subtle and hidden calls to think again about how design can create an immanent space of encounter with content, not just play the role of neutral container.

Atonality

Speaking of the relationship between music and language, Adorno states that music, along with syntax, and formal structures, employs "a temporal sequence of articulated sounds which are more than just sounds."[10] Unlike language, music does not possess an external 'signified' and in this sense, music remains non-conceptual. Adorno points out the non-identical nature of music and language: Music and language, while possessing similar attributes, divide along the fault-line of "intentionality", or instrumentality. However, he goes on to say that albeit specific concepts may not emerge from tonality, still a kind of spaciality can be articulated. This spatiality is shown by repetitive sequences, and harmonic figures which reappear, and become, as he puts it, 'universal ciphers'. Adorno suggests further that when contextualized, these figures and sequences in turn provide a certain kind of space. Thus he writes:

10. T. W. Adorno, *Music and Language: A Fragment, Quasi una Fantasia, Essays on Modern Music*, Theodor W. Adorno. Trans Rodney Livingstone, (Verso, London, New York: 2012), 1.

> "Space for musical specificity, just as concepts do for a particular reality, and at the same time, as with language, their abstractness [is] redeemed by the context in which they [are] located. The only difference is that the identity of these musical concepts [lies] in their own nature and not in a signified outside them."[11]

In a somewhat similar vein, one could characterise Nietzsche's re-staging of philology as emulating or, indeed being considered, a kind of 'musical event,' where the lyrical timbre of his pacings, punctuations and arguments allowed one to understand the nuance of an argument by treating philology 'musically'.[12] Another way of saying this might be that language is to be viewed as an instrument, rather than as instrumental, one that we must to learn to play well.

In a related but different sense, Andrei Igamberdiev, speaking of Beethoven's *Grosse Fugue* begins to develop the relation of text to dissonance and dissonance to the double fugue. Described in its own time as 'incomprehensible', the Grosse Fugue challenged the prevailing musical canons. The Fugue's dark, complex tones and lack of harmonic resolution, are singularly uncompromised and complex. As a piece of music, which actively embraces counterpoint, and which consists of multiple movements within a single large movement, Stravinsky called it "an absolutely contemporary piece of music that will be contemporary forever."[13]

The linguistic analogy could be made through conversation, where elements enter and depart with extreme suddenness, the composer / performer adding and subtracting fragments from the main theme at breakneck speed and in multiple layers and in plural times. The word Fugue comes from the Latin 'to flee' and the 'event', where sudden, unexpected, changes and shifts in the movement of the music are the motor-force. The *Grosse Fugue* is incomplete, self-referential, and recursive; its form and structure is neither finite nor expressly infinite, but the tension between the two keeps the movement and dynamic of the music alive, just as the tension between the dynamics of white space, typography and their counterpoint rhythms keeps the page alive.[14]

---

11. Ibid., 2.

12. Friedrich Nietzsche, *Diaries* B. 3, 257; Dec. 21, 1871. See in particular where he writes: "Everything that [...] cannot be understood in relation to music engenders [...] downright aversion and disgust in me." Cited in Rüdiger Safranski, *Nietzsche: A Philosophical Biography*, 2002 (W. W. Norton, USA), 19.

13. Igor Stravinsky and Robert Craft, Dialogues and a Diary (New York: Doubleday, 1963), 24.

14. Jan Tschichold, having set in motion the precepts for an entirely new form of modernist typography in his book *Asymmetric Typography*, (Faber, 1967), which was considered highly radical at that time, stated: 'White space is to be regarded as an active element, not a passive background,'. However, he returned in the late 1930s to the classical, symmetrical canon of typographic design, subsequently

This is precisely what we have tried to generate within the two different bounded bodies of Zētēsis, Vol. 1 ~ a way of writing, and indeed reading, that is closer to music ~ a kind of dark fugue ~ rather than to writing per se. For the classical canon has the capacity to be cruel, to be the enemy of the arts, to be an omnipotent 'mop' of creative juices; upholding tidiness as though the same as rigorous experimentation; or complete transparency as equivalent to communication. This is particularly the case with certain kinds of design ~ where the canon can belie or smother certain forms of thought, imagination, originality and understanding through a kind of generic massification of well-trodden typographic paths that feign openness, but instead can amass a whole series of judgments that quietly weigh on any interpretative reading.

However, as design is also always a collaborator in thought, and practice, ~ a partner in meaning, a vital organ in the body of this book ~ there has been an opportunity to seek out the (sometimes) illusive openings where we can begin a rewriting of the canon in the most sensitive of ways. To design within the odd, new parameters that Zētēsis has demanded, has required a particular turn to the carnal connections of the body, a connection formed through a fundamental *knowing* of rhythm: to move through choreographed pages, each one an attempt at conveying not only information and concept of the research to hand, but the rhythmic experience of postulating time, timing, and temporally induced spaces. For on the stage created by 'the book', there is no page considered in isolation. The publication in its entirety is a continuous stream of coming and goings, of concepts, remarks, events, just past, just present, just about-to-happen.

This design-concept of rhythm is one that negates repetitive sameness as its principle concern. We would like to suggest that an 'atonal' rhythm is required, one that is similarly comprised of repeating elements (as is the necessity of 'the book' as collective material), but one that is given freedom in the spaces around these elements. Here, edges are no longer considered as rigid structure and the distance in between is no longer confined to the regular beat of the interval. We might image this as a camouflage pattern, which by its very nature is ideal for the inconspicuous inserting of subverted elements.

To understand design in this way is, in the same breath, to understand design in harmonious coexistence with canonical thought. Just as a grouping of sounds is not dictated by the relation between sounds, so too the formation of design elements is not dictated with purely self-referential consideration. An atonal rhythm is made manifest by one that must dance always at its side.

---

expounding the virtues of classicism in both typography and page layout. He later worked for Penguin Publishing. See also *The Form of the Book, Essays on the Morality of Good Design* (Hartley & Marks, 1996). Tschichold was described as an 'apostate' for having initially championed and then rejected the 'New Typography' as it had become known.

The canonical rhythms that refer to the accumulated knowledge of thousands of years of historical and cultural progress in design are not only present, but essential to the cohesion of otherwise decontextualized elements. Intelligent listening and active participation is required in the formation of a structure that is to call itself 'rhythmic',[15] without the canon there is no communal dialogue, there can be no space to experience the 'beat'.

This ensemble of writing / reading / listening existing as it does, linked together by a variety of voices, is presented with an atonal beat layered as a participant in the subversion of existing patterns ~ a kind of atonality that flows throughout as a slightly roguish disturber of the peace. There are places within the design where elements have been toppled, snapped and flourished in new ways to cloud Warde's infamous crystal goblet; to give the musculature of design its visibility without disrupting the necessary comfort zones too much.[16] It may simply be a 'backwards' page number or an irregular alignment of titles; one might follow the line of a lowercase g, its tail flowing ana-fractuously from its body, and be made aware of a unique eccentricity in the form of its upward-curved ear, a single horn protruding from its head. It is in this world that we operate.

Atonal design: it requires more than an audacious dive into uncharted and possibly murky 'uncommunicative' waters; it has required us to dance within and from the singular-plurality, to recall Jean-Luc Nancy, of rhythm.[17]

Sheena Calvert & Joseph Bisat Marshall

---

15. Dr. Mark Walker in conversation with Joseph Bisat Marshall, 16th September 2013.

16. Op. cit. B. Warde, *The Crystal Goblet*.

17. Jean-Luc Nancy, *Being Singular Plural*, (Stanford University Press, 2004). Jean-luc Nancy poses a new relation of the 'I' to the 'we', once drawn out through the nuances of the hyphen: "Being singular plural: in a single stroke, without punctuation, without a mark of equivalence, implication, or sequence. A single, continuous-discontinuous mark tracing out the entirety of the ontological domain, being-with-itself designated as the "with" of being, of the singular and plural, and dealing a blow to ontology—not only another signification but also another syntax. The "meaning of Being": not only as the "meaning of with," but also, and above all, as the "with" of meaning. Because none of these three terms precedes or grounds the other, each designates the co-essence of the others. This co-essence puts essence itself in the hyphenation ~ "being-singular-plural" ~ which is a mark of union and also a mark of division, a mark of sharing that effaces itself, leaving each term to its isolation and its being-with-the-others", 37.
We might therefore ask, what is the plural of rhythm, and what is its singular?

Virgil W. Brower taught Ethics at the Chicago Police Academy and is currently Full-Time Lecturer of Philosophy at Chicago State University, where he teaches Logic, Ethics, Critical Theory, and Comparative Religion. He is a double doctoral candidate in the Theology, Ethics, and Human Sciences division of The Chicago Theological Seminary and the Program in Comparative Literary Studies at Northwestern University, where he co-directs The Paul of Tarsus Interdisciplinary Working Group. www.northwestern.academia.edu/virgilbrower

Sheena Calvert is a typographer, designer and philosopher She holds an MA in Fine Art and Design from Yale University, and an AHRC funded PhD in Philosophy and Aesthetics from The University of Greenwich. Her research is concerned with rethinking the relationship between language and meaning, viewed through the lens[es] of identity / difference, and paradox. She is particularly interested in how a form of immanent textual 'performativity', undertaken through typography, might amplify philosophical content. She teaches practice and theory of design at Central St. Martins, and The University of Westminster. 'materialanguage' is her most current research project, which explores language and its relationship to materiality as it pertains to the production of thought / power / subjectivity / time / sensuality.

Meryl Donoghue is an internationally renowned artist. She holds an MA in Fine Art from the Slade School of Fine Art, University College London, and a first first-class honours degree in Fine Art from Bath Spa University (2007). She was awarded the University Prize for her final show. Having no fixed medium, Meryl moves from delicate pencil drawings to highly augmented photographic prints, and from experimenting with sound and animation to installations comprising animatronics and taxidermy. Her work borders on the sinister and the bizarre, exploring concerns relating to self-constructed reality, childhood, adolescence, sexuality, exile, isolation, loss and death. www.meryldonoghue.com

Norbert Finzsch is Professor of North American History at the University of Cologne. He specializes in the history of racisms, sexualities and corporealities. www.aaa.phil-fak.uni-koeln.de/8825.html?&L=1

Johnny Golding is a philosopher. Her books, videos, philosophic-sound installations and stage productions cover the complex intersections of fine art, ethics, sexualities and physics. Foregrounding synesthetic materiality, fractal patterning, camouflage, curved-time dimension, much of her recent work continues to be filtered through the parrhēsiastic ethics of the flesh, borrowing from feminism, queer studies and the wild sciences. Director of The Centre for Fine Art Research (CFAR) at the Birmingham Institute of Art & Design (BCU); Executive Editor of *Zētēsis*, she holds the Chair as Research Professor of Philosophy & Fine Art at the School of Art-BIAD (Margaret St). www.bcu.ac.uk/BIAD/research/people/research-staff/johnny-sue-golding; www.bcu.academia.edu/ProfJohnnyGolding

Stephen Kennedy's research interests lie at the intersection of theory and practice in relation to the political economy of contemporary communications technology. A DJ and composer, his most current work, Chaos Media (Bloomsbury, 2014) seeks to develop the paradigmatic tools for contemporary, cultural research based on sonic rather than visual methodologies. Director, Institute for Contemporary Culture and Aesthetics (ICAS) at the University of Greenwich. www.gre.academia.edu/stephenkennedy

Hannah Lammin is an artist and philosopher whose work choreographs the complex and politically decadent landscapes of place, voice and identity in the theatre of contemporary sociality. An AHRC award holder, she is currently finishing her PhD at BIAD, Birmingham City University. www.gre.academia.edu/HannahLammin

Sarah Mann-O'Donnell is a doctoral candidate at Northwestern University, Chicago. Currently studying in Paris under the Northwestern University-Paris Program, where she was awarded a major research fellowship in Critical Theory. Her dissertation, *Erotic Patience: Thinking Convalescence with Nietzsche, Proust, and Deleuze*, examines tensions of patience and longing in philosophico-literary representations of convalescence. Her most recent research, "*Convalescence retrouvée: Proustian patients of anticipation*," was selected and presented at the 2013 ACLA (University of Toronto: 2013). www.angelskinned.wordpress.com

Joseph Bisat Marshall is a London based designer, currently studying at Central St. Martins, University of the Arts London. His work traverses multiple aspects of design, from theatre to the printed page. His design work for the stage includes the UK tour of *Oliver!* (2011-13), *Miss Saigon* in Utrecht and Tokyo (2012) and London's West End (2014), *Barnum* at Chichester Festival Theatre (2013), and the US tour of *Phantom of the Opera* (2013-2014). Much of Joseph's design research output concerns contemporary philosophy, particularly the analytic / linguistic notions of experience and the question of the 'ineffable narrative' as the odd, seductive and extra-representational distance between the two. www.josephbisatmarshall.co.uk

Mattia Paganelli is an artist and philosopher whose research combines complexity theory with epistemological issues in representation, discursive and visual environments. Having exhibited widely, his art practice incorporates a variety of media / mediated technologies, live interventions and imaging, articulating how sense emerges from process rather than being represented through it. Currently an AHRC PhD candidate in Philosophy at the Centre for Fine art Research (CFAR), The School of Art, BCU. He holds a distinction in Philosophy from Universtà degli Studi di Milano, and a double MA in Fine Art (Chelsea College of Art, UAL) and Media Arts Philosophy (Greenwich). Mattia is also a member of the collective blog nazioneindiana.com where he publishes regularly. www.cfar-biad.co.uk/index.php/researchers?id=326

Henry Rogers is an artist-researcher at the Centre for Fine Art Research (CFAR) at the School of Art, Birmingham Institute of Art and Design, BCU. An internationally exhibited painter as well as author of several books and monographs, he is a PhD supervisor, Director of the Arts Based Masters Programme and Course Director of the internationally renowned MA Fine Art and the internationally unique MA Queer Studies in Arts and Culture. www.bcu.ac.uk/BIAD/research/people/research-staff/henry-rogers

Daniel Rubinstein is an artist, critical theorist and writer whose research is concerned with the relationship between visual culture, new media and philosophy. Underpinned by multifaceted engagement with photography, his work examines the digital image in the context of networked and mediated urban environments. Awarded his doctorate for his work on the latent image (BIAD-BCU: 2013), he is the editor of the international, peer-reviewed journal *Philosophy of Photography*. His latest co-authored book is an edited anthology *On the Verge of Photography; Imaging beyond Representation*. Daniel is the head of MA Photography at Central Saint Martins. www.csm-arts.academia.edu/DrDanielRubinstein

Lynn Turner has published on deconstruction and animals, feminism, science fiction and visual culture in journals such as *Humanimalia, Mosaic: journal for the interdisciplinary study of literature*, *Camera Obscura*, and *Derrida Today*. She is the co-editor of a special issue of parallax called *'bon appétit'* (2013) and the editor of *The Animal Question in Deconstruction* (2013). She is Lecturer in Visual Culture, Goldsmiths, University of London. www.gold.ac.uk/visual-cultures/l-turner/

Mark Walker was awarded his Doctorate in Philosophy (2008) on the work of Theodor Adorno. His major interests remain focussed on the philosophical concerns of Adorno. www.cfar-biad.co.uk

Perry Zurn is a doctoral candidate in philosophy at DePaul University, Chicago. Zurn's research concerns contemporary French philosophy, social and political philosophy, and ethics. www.depaul.academia.edu/PerryZurn

Zētēsis: research generated by curiosity.

Journal for the Intersecting Fine Art, Philosophy
and the Wild Sciences.

Vol. 1, No. 1: The Cruelty of the Classical Canon.
ISBN 978-1-873352-06-9

Zētēsis: research generated by curiosity is an international research journal that welcomes experimental, provocative and critical engagement with the intersecting landscapes of fine art, philosophy, cultural practice and the wild sciences. Foregrounding this intersection, Zētēsis invites artists, philosophers, cultural theorists and scientists to consider the ethical, political and aesthetic impact emerging from the advances in contemporary physics, meta-mathematics, queer theory, morphogenesis, feminist ecologies, and all types of 'thinking machines' ~ artificially intelligent or otherwise ~ on everyday life.

The School of Art and its Centre for Fine Art Research (CFAR) at The Birmingham Institute for Art & Design is one of the world-class rated research environments and provides intellectual, practical and financial support for Zētēsis. All research published in this journal goes through the standard peer-review process supported by its International Advisory Board of scholars and artists in the field, as listed overleaf. Published via ARTicle Press (www.articlepress.co.uk), it is dedicated to making high quality research publicly available at point of publication (Gold Standard). As a result, each individual research piece is available immediately / at point of publication in a dedicated online arena, called The Reading Room (www.zetesis.co.uk/TheReadingRoom). Should one wish to have an individual copy of an article, this may be purchased as a down-loadable print-on-demand piece. Each volume is also available for purchase in designated bookstores and galleries or online.

Contributions:

Enquiries and submissions are encouraged from any scholar / artists / practitioners, whose work engages with the concerns of this journal. Each journal volume will address a particular set of themes, for which a call will be placed via www.zetesis.co.uk inviting submissions. Prospective Guest Editors are welcome to approach the Editors with their proposal by email. Please submit all enquiries to TheEditors@zetesis.co.uk.

Format for Article Submissions:

Articles will normally range from 3500-7500 words, including footnotes, but excluding the author's abstract and keywords. Short papers should range between 500-3500 words. Conference and book reviews should range between 1000-2000 words.

Footnotes and References:

Explanatory / referential footnotes are particularly encouraged. To this end, all written work should follow the Chicago referencing style. As all written work will be submitted for peer review, please submit two word files (.docx or similar) of an article or artwork, with one version excluding all personal information. Images must be submitted in high resolution (300dpi), in TIFF format when possible. Copyright clearance is the responsibility of the contributor. For detailed instruction on submission style please see: www.zetesis.co.uk

Format for Visual and Media Submissions:

All images must be submitted in high resolution (300 dpi) and in TIFF format when possible. Copyright clearance is the responsibility of the contributor. Moving image / sound pieces will be published on the ARTicle press website linked to the volume of the journal to which it is a part.

All Correspondence should be sent in the first instance to:

Snail: The Editors
Zetesis
The School of Art,
Margaret Street,
Birmingham,
B3 3BX
United Kingdom

Email: TheEditors@zetesis.co.uk

Price: £10 per volume.

ARTicle Press   BIRMINGHAM CITY University   Birmingham Institute of Art and Design   CFAR The Centre for Fine Art Research

Zētēsis: research generated by curiosity

Executive Editor:

Johnny Golding, Director, Centre for Fine Art Research (CFAR)

Editorial Board:

Mona Casey, David Cheeseman, Johnny Golding, James Hellings,
Mattia Paganelli, Henry Rogers, Carol Wild, Grace Williams

Research Arts Editors:

Mattia Paganelli, Grace Williams

Designers:

Sheena Calvert & Joseph Bisat Marshall

Images by Meryl Donoghue. Front cover: *Ten for the Devils Own Self* (2008), *One For Sorrow* (2007), *Regrettee Norm* (2007), *Guilt is a Terrible Ghost* (2007); Each 170cm x 130cm; mounted Giclée prints courtesy of the artist.

Zētēsis

Research Generated by Curiosity

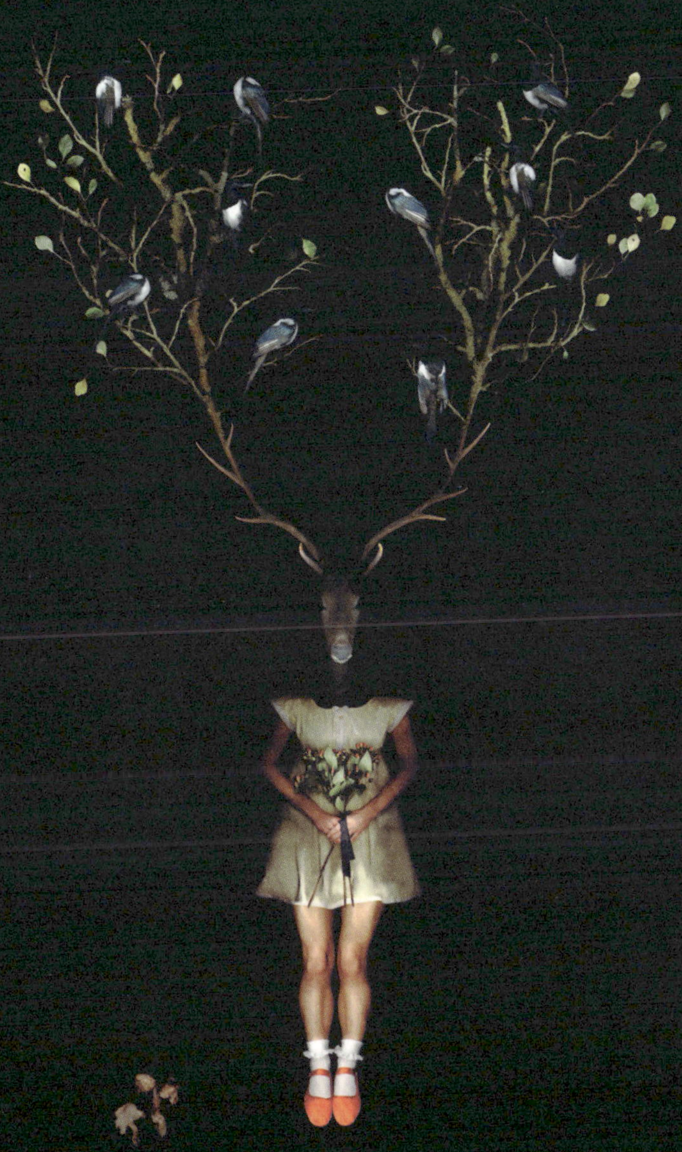

The Cruelty of the Classical Canon

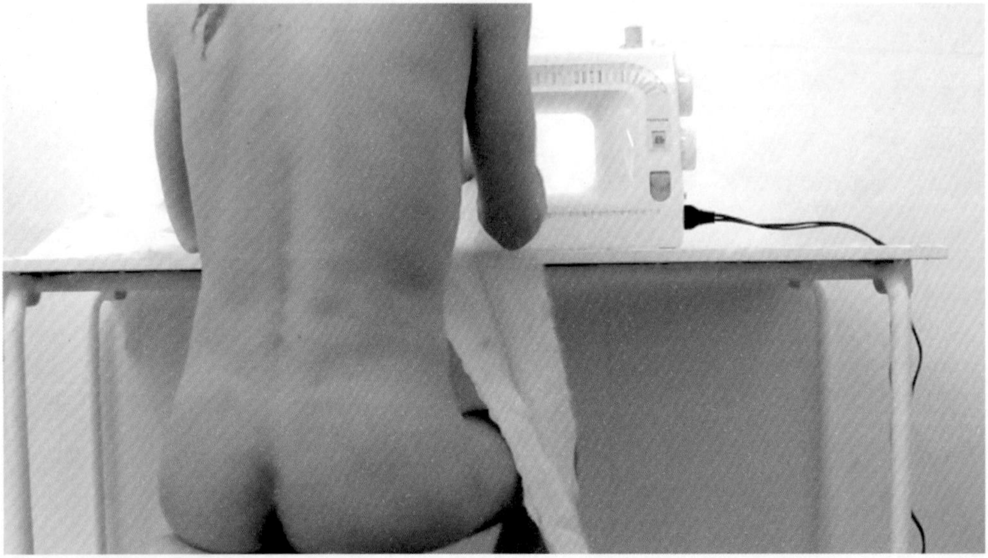

Kręć się, kręc wrzeciono,
prysła wątła nić,
wstydem dziewczę plonie,
wstydź się, dziewczę, wstydź!

(S. Moniuszko, Przasniczka)

'talepiej' stills from the video *Scissors and the Myth of Gender* by Jakub Ceglarz (2013).

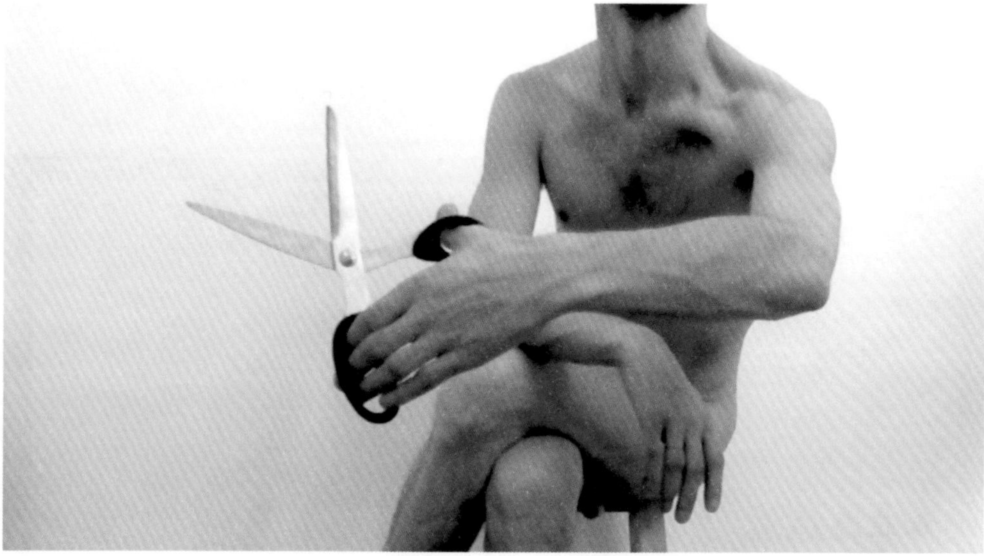

Turn up, turn up the spundle,
burst the frail thread,
girl burns with shame,
shame on you, girl, shame!

(S. Moniuszko, Przasniczka

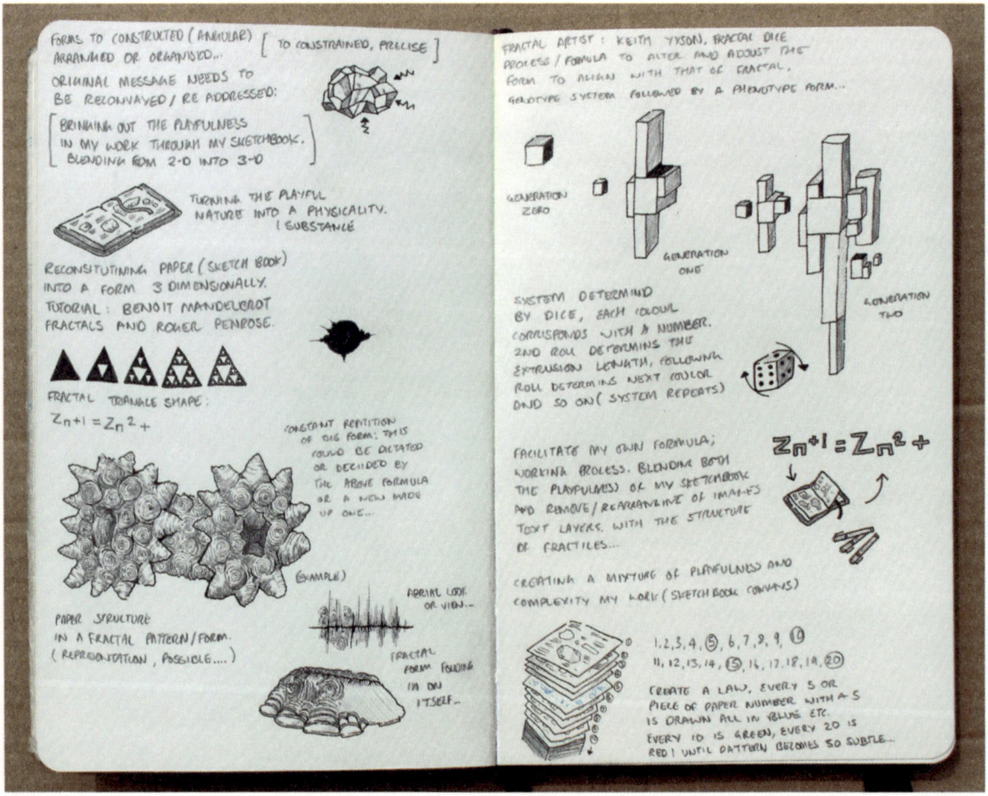
FORMS TO CONSTRUCTED (ANGULAR) ARRANGED OR ORGANISED...
[TO CONSTRAINED, PRECISE]
ORIGINAL MESSAGE NEEDS TO BE RECONVAYED / RE ADDRESSED:
[BRINGING OUT THE PLAYFULNESS IN MY WORK THROUGH MY SKETCHBOOK. BLENDING FROM 2-D INTO 3-D]
TURNING THE PLAYFUL NATURE INTO A PHYSICALITY. / SUBSTANCE
RECONSITUTING PAPER (SKETCH BOOK) INTO A FORM 3 DIMENSIONALLY.
TUTORIAL: BENOIT MANDELBROT FRACTALS AND ROGER PENROSE.
FRACTAL TRIANGLE SHAPE:
Zn+1 = Zn 2 +
CONSTANT REPITITION OF THE FORM: THIS COULD BE DICTATED OR DECIDED BY THE ABOVE FORMULA OR A NEW MADE UP ONE...
(EXAMPLE)
AERIAL LOOK OR VIEW...
PAPER STRUCTURE IN A FRACTAL PATTERN/FORM. (REPRESENTATION, POSSIBLE....)
FRACTAL FORM FOLDING IN ON ITSELF...
FRACTAL ARTIST: KEITH YYSON, FRACTAL DICE PROCESS / FORMULA TO ALTER AND ADJUST THE FORM TO ALIGN WITH THAT OF FRACTAL,
GENOTYPE SYSTEM FOLLOWED BY A PHENOTYPE FORM...
GENERATION ZERO
GENERATION ONE
GENERATION TWO
SYSTEM DETERMIND BY DICE, EACH COLOUR CORRISPONDS WITH A NUMBER. 2ND ROLL DETERMINS THE EXTRUSION LENGTH, FOLLOWING ROLL DETERMINS NEXT COLOR AND SO ON (SYSTEM REPEATS)
FACILITATE MY OWN FORMULA; WORKING PROCESS. BLENDING BOTH THE PLAYFULNESS OF MY SKETCHBOOK AND REMOVE/REARRANGING OF IMAGES TEXT LAYERS. WITH THE STRUCTURE OF FRACTILES...
Zn+1 = Zn2 +
CREATING A MIXTURE OF PLAYFULNESS AND COMPLEXITY MY WORK (SKETCH BOOK CANVAS)
1, 2, 3, 4, 5, 6, 7, 8, 9, 10
11, 12, 13, 14, 15, 16, 17, 18, 19, 20
CREATE A LAW, EVERY 5 OR PIECE OF PAPER NUMBER WITH A 5 IS DRAWN ALL IN BLUE ETC. EVERY 10 IS GREEN, EVERY 20 IS RED! UNTIL PATTERN BECOMES SO SUBTLE...

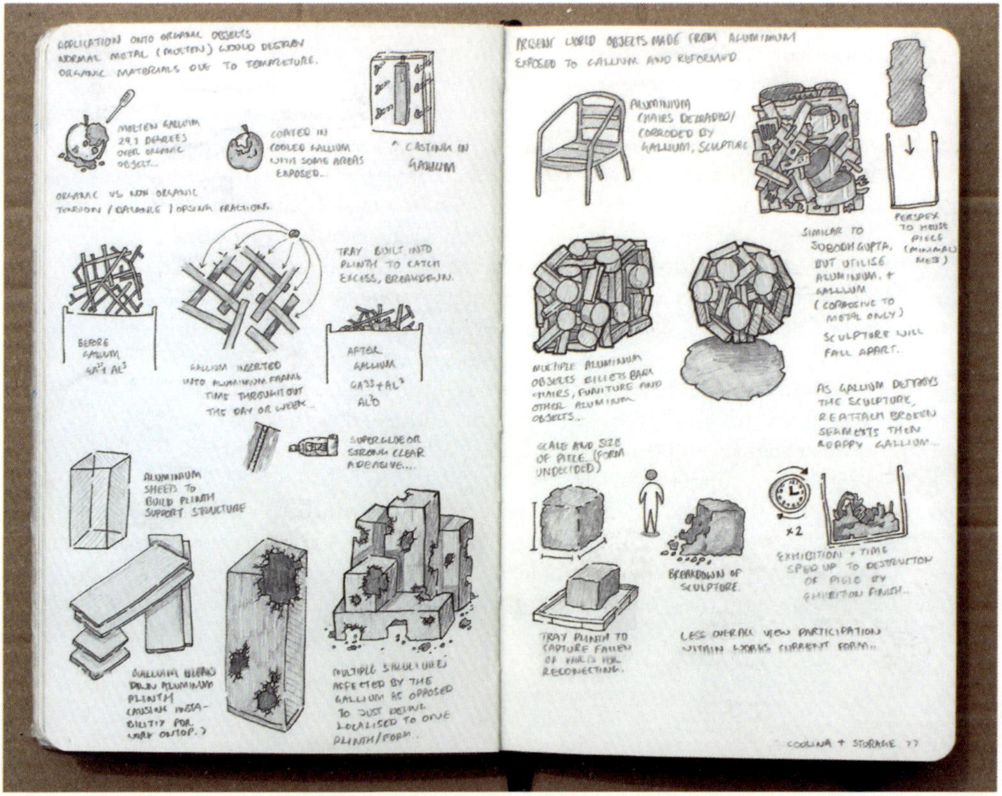

The final form(s) emerging out of these few pages shown here will be built from a composite wood material made from the sketchbook pages themselves, organized and layered according to the imaginary and irrational with mathematical formulation. This form will then be subjected to large currents of electricity causing natural fractal patterns to appear over its surface. It just might work.

My Body is Your Body

For over a decade, AMAE has been investigating, through their art practice, the representation of the psychological tension that is created in the body that results from the influences of society. Their work also explores the theory of the Self, the perception of sexuality and the therapeutic influence of art in the construction of identity. In 2012, AMAE presented as a live stream broadcast, I Will Jump First, a Male to Female Sexual Reassignment Operation by Italian duo AMAE.

For many artists their muses were the source of their inspiration and even the object of their desire and dreams. For AMAE the muse is a woman in a man's body. Gaia grew up in a male body never thinking about herself as a man. As soon as she took her first steps she was rejected by the company who had up to that point, employed her. Gaia is now 37 and she is still contemplating a sex change. Gaia is one person of many in this situation. AMAE felt close to her feelings and wanted to explore those feelings in a way that might develop / represent a merger between the artist and the muse. Many questions arise from this kind of artistic coupling, addressed as they have been at the point of genitalia and skin. Where will these identities lead in their support of each other?

Now the time has come to give Gaia a hand and say: 'I will jump first'. Photographic slices from this live performance tries to get at the heart of getting a 'Male to Female Sexual Reassignment' broadcast in real time from the wood workshop of The Birmingham School of Art.

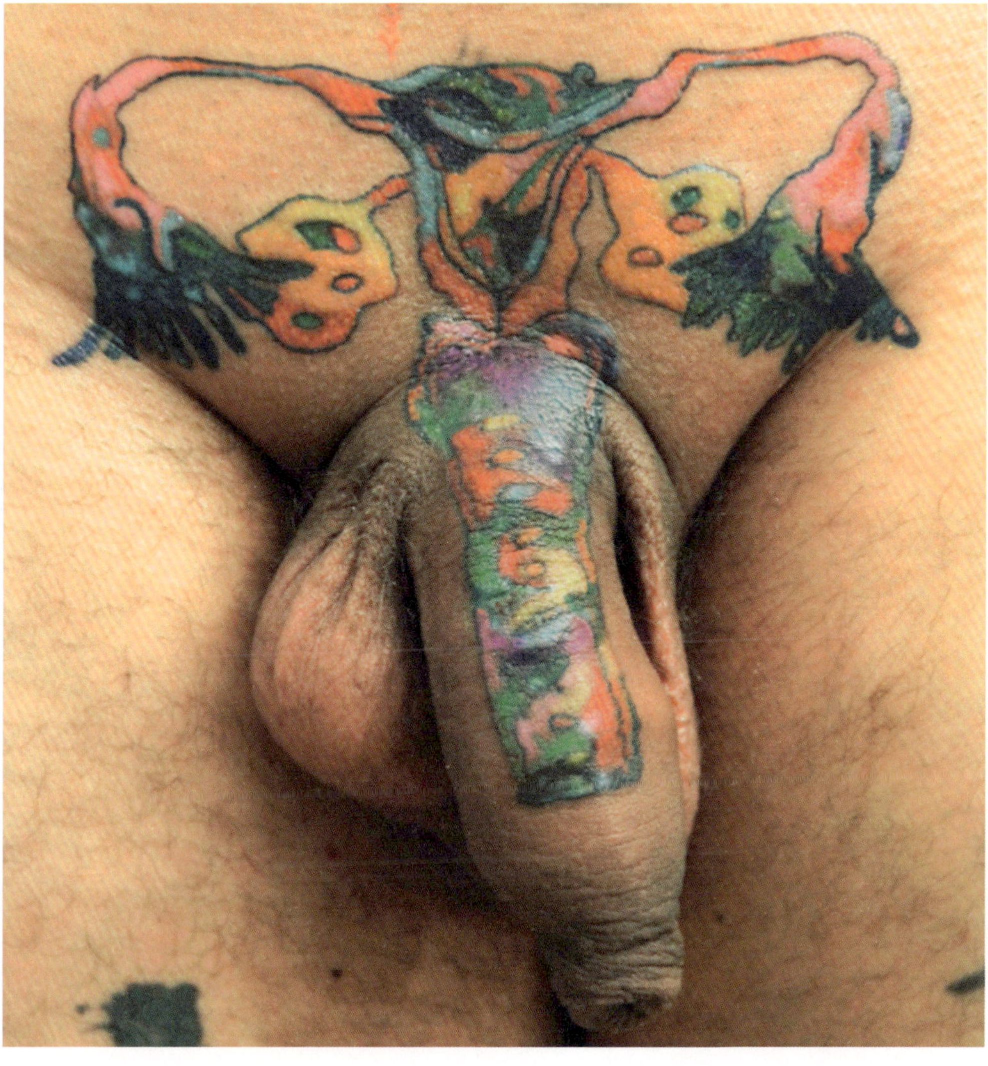

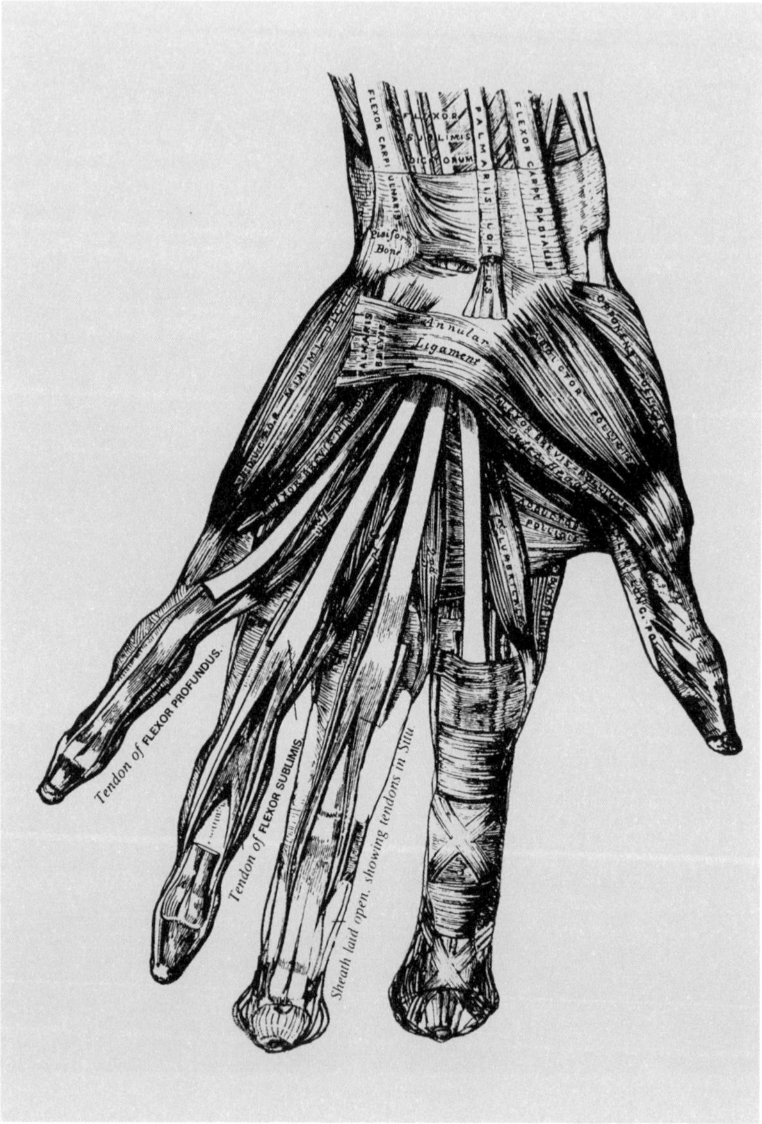

Lesbian Genitalia (2013).

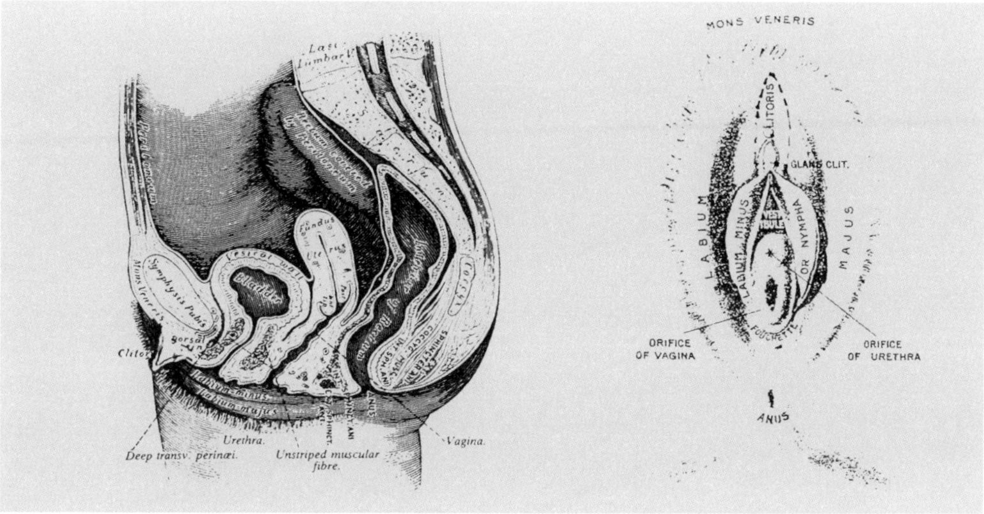

"Clitoromegaly" in Hannah Honeywill, *Queer Anatomy (dis-organ-ised bodies): A queering* of *Gray's* Anatomy (2012).

Dyke: a slang term for lesbian, often used as an insult but has been reclaimed by some parts of the lesbian community as an empowered term of identification.

Butch: a lesbian woman who is more comfortable with masculine gender codes, styles or identities than with feminine ones.

Stone Butch: is a dyke (lesbian) placed somewhere on the boundary between female masculinity and transgender subjectivity. During sex they are active but don't like to be touched and possibly will remain clothed.

Femme (also referred to as Lipstick Lesbian): takes on the traditional female gender role, simultaneously identifying as a lesbian.

Tomboy: connotes boyishness within women/girls, both within heterosexual and homosexual context.

Lesbian Body: a polymorphous body: the global disparity between social constructs and environments which have a rhizomatic impact on what and how a lesbian body is and becomes.

Androgynous: represents some version of gender mixing.

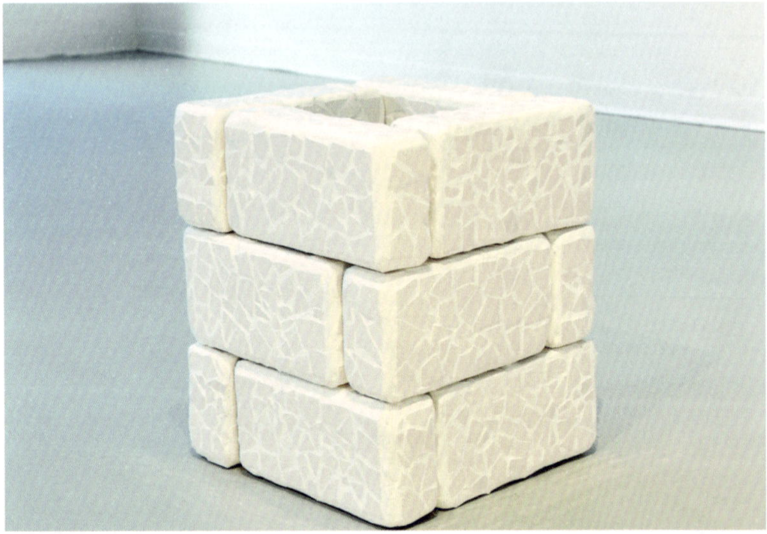

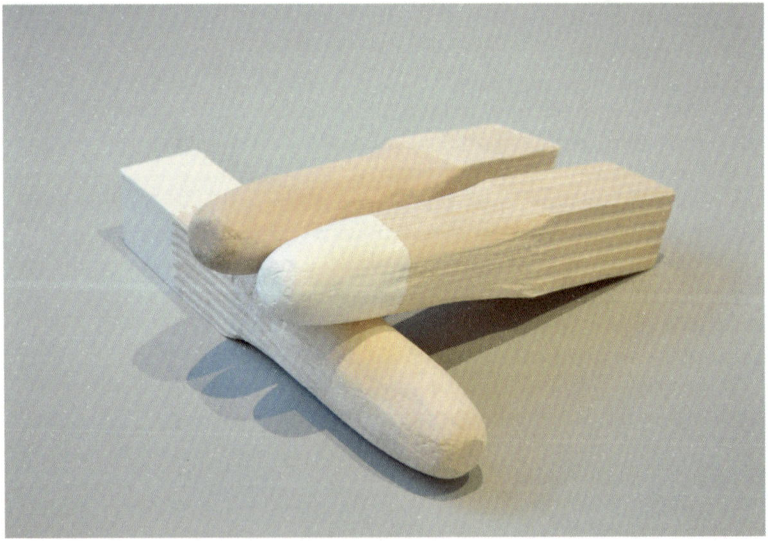

"He sees mountains as mountains, but it does not follow that he sees them as mountains just as he saw them before." ~ Arthur Danto, *The Transfiguration of the Commonplace: A Philosophy of Art*, (1983).

Extremely Precise Objects of Ambiguous Use[1]

For me, the creation and sustenance of an increased variety of genders is a question of transforming matter. In one sense, this transformation could refer to the cosmetic, surgical, and hormonal interventions by which transgender and gender-variant people literally change their bodies. But, gender variant people also engage in another type of material transformation that is not visible in the manner of these types of physical procedures. Bodies and body parts change, but not objectively. Your breasts are still there, but they are no longer feminine ~ they are your chest. Your penis is a large clitoris. Your husky voice is no longer a male signifier. Your body is the same, but in crucial ways it has changed. These types of changes are a question of belief. Belief in a *material* form. They are about the creation of new modes of perception by which the same thing appears completely different. These bodies are a mixture of the real and the virtual, where realness is virtual, virtuality is real. What Brian Massumi calls, after Foucault, "incorporeal materialism."[2] These bodies are both real *and* imaginary ~ fleshy reinterpretations of the gendered significance of their physical parts. Transforming gender is a question of transforming matter, but, more than that, it is a question of how we understand what matter is, especially the matter that is our physical bodies. Gayle Salamon, reads transgender through the lens of the philosophy of Merleau-Ponty. She describes the body in general, but the transgender body in particular as "a mixture or amalgam of substance and ideal located somewhere between its objectively quantifiable materiality and its phantasmatic extensions into the world."[3] Or, as Merleau-Ponty asks: "Is my body a thing, is it an idea?"[4] Is there a way to understand materiality that can account for the complex relationships between the real and the imaginary proposed by gender-variant bodies? What is it when a body looks exactly the same but has transformed into something completely different?

1. This is an excerpt from a much longer essay: "Extremely Precise Objects of Ambiguous Use," paper presented at the School of Art, Institute of Chicago, MFA Exhibition 14 May 2011. See http://www.rehgordon.net.

2. Brian Massumi, *Parables for the Virtual: Movement, Affect, Sensation*, (Durham / London: Duke University Press, 2002), 5.

3. Gayle Salamon, *Assuming a Body: Transgender and Rhetorics of Materiality*, (New York: Columbia Univ Press, 2010), 64-65.

4. Maurice Merleau-Ponty, "The Intertwining ~ The Chiasm," in *The Visible and the Invisible*, trans Alphonso Lingus, (Evanston: Northwestern University Press), 152.

The Rootless Forest

If the soil beneath our feet shifts, what happens when that foundation erodes and in its wake, our home, our country, our hopes shift with it? These, in the context of violence and war, were the questions that prompted this project.

In war, landscapes people and communities are altered, resulting in families being relocated. The Rootless Forest is a literal and metaphorical platform that gives voice to communities affected by conflict, inspiring new narratives for landscapes that are foreign and local at the same time. During the journey the boat broadcasted a soundscape, consisting of verbatim stories from people affected by the current Afghan conflict, including UK military personnel who have served overseas and Afghans who have settled in Birmingham as a result of war in their homeland. As The Rootless Forest moves slowly along the water, its continual motion poetically echoed these accounts of displacement and relocation. The Rootless Forest reflects upon the upheaval experienced by communities, individuals and landscapes in times of conflict. Inspired by the moving forest of Birnham Wood in Shakespeare's Macbeth, the trees were a motif for both camouflage and combat, a habitat for multiple voices and a transitional space between past and future.

The Rootless Forest existed as a mobile artwork, weighing over 20 tonnes, with 100 trees up to 3 meters tall planted along its 16 metre length. This mini-forest travelled at walking pace along the Birmingham and Black Country Canals, with recorded stories about passage, change and home, told by families from the military, and UK Afghan communities in Birmingham. The trees ~ all native to the UK, including alder and birch ~ are to be re-planted in Walsall Arboretum on completion of the project to become a lasting monument to those affected by conflict.

The Rootless Forest was developed by Beth Derbyshire, Wheatley Fellow at Birmingham Institute of Art and Design. Funded by the Arts Council, England and supported by the School of Art at the Birmingham Institute for Art & Design (BIAD) Birmingham City University, The Centre for Fine Art Research (CFAR) and the Canal & River Trust. The soundscape was a collaboration between artist Beth Derbyshire and voice director, Dr Tara McAllister-Viel.

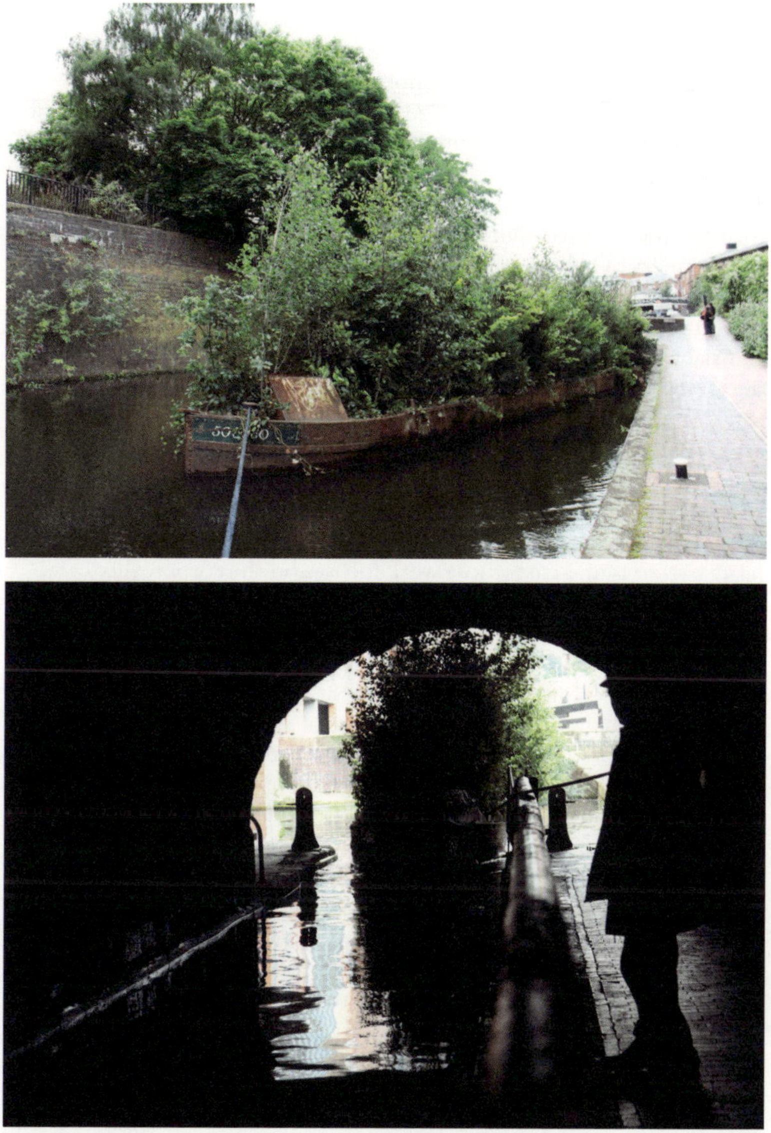

The Rootless Forest, a moving landscape and soundscape, (2012-2013).

AMAE, as a collaborative singularity, focuses on the tensions generated in marginalised bodies by heteronormative society. AMAE's research contaminates traditional languages of art communication (poetry, video, sound, photography, installation, performance) with mass media via photographic works and performances, which are often broadcast live on the web. Working on international platforms across the EU, AMAE focuses on intersubjectivity and transfer in performance art; inheritance and mimicry of behaviour; mimicry against emulation; identification and conflict; primary society and contemporary society; time and space of assimilation of empathetic behaviours; behaviours towards otherness; transient bodies; augmented reality. The aim of the current research, 58 (+1) indices on the body (working with philosopher Jean-Luc Nancy) is to consider emulation as a mimicry of transit within performance art, deepening the question of identification and conflict via live audience interaction and guided by Nancy's philosophical approach to the body. www.amae-art.com

Jakub Ceglarz is an artist whose work focuses on the corporeality of sense, text, sexuality, dis / placement and its influence in art. His artistic practices play with the technological and epistemological dilemmas in photography, video, and sculpture. Originally from Poland, he holds a BA in Fine Art from Middlesex University and an MA in Fine Art from Birmingham City University, where he received first prize for outstanding work. He will commence a PhD at the School of Art / Birmingham Institute for Art & Design, BCU, primarily focussing on the palimpsest. www.kubaceglarz.blogspot.co.uk

Beth Derbyshire is currently Research Fellow at the Centre for Fine Art Research (CFAR), Birmingham Institute of Art and Design, BCU. She holds a BA from Ruskin, Oxford and an MFA from Chelsea College of Art, University of the Arts London. Her work primarily focuses on public art involving local, regional and national communities, including the hearing impaired, refugees, veterans, and the military. Major projects with over one million visitors include: *Anthem* (Eden Project: 2009), *Seven Seas* (Project Ocean-Selfridges: 2011), and *Rootless Forest* (Arts Council of England: 2012), the latter of which was launched along the Birmingham canals and gave voice to the complex narratives of both

Afghani refugees and British servicemen. Derbyshire's latest project, *The Ark* (commissioned by Creativity Works), is a floating sculpture / cinema travelling along regional canals in order to bring contemporary art to a public sector not often reached by gallery exhibition alone. www.bethderbyshire.com

Gordon Hall is an artist and writer based in New York. Gordon has exhibited and performed in such venues as SculptureCenter (NYC), The Kitchen (NYC), Taxter and Spengemann (NYC), Samson Projects (Boston), LaMontagne Gallery (Boston), Roots and Culture (Chicago), Western Exhibitions (Chicago), Gallery 400 @ the University of Illinois Chicago, and The Museum of Contemporary Art (Chicago). Gordon has been published in *Critical Correspondance*, *Monsters and Dust*, *New York Art Magazine*, *Title Magazine*, *Make Literary Magazine*, and was the curator of Second Gallery in Boston (2005-2007). Currently the Director of the Center for Experimental Lectures hosted by MOMA PS1 in Queens, NY. Gordon holds an MA in Visual and Critical Studies and a MFA in Fiber and Material Studies from School of the Art Institute of Chicago, and teaches at Parsons the New School for Design. www.gordonhall.net

Hannah Honeywill is a Birmingham based artist. The key concerns of her research and practice are negotiating and re-presenting queer bodies. Hannah has a degree in sculpture from Camberwell College of Arts in London and an MA in Fine Art from The School of Art, Birmingham Institute of Art and Design, BCU. In 2012 she was selected for the Art Laguna sculpture prize in Venice and in 2011 The Threadneedle Prize in London. She will begin her PhD research in January 2014 on female piracy and the body. www.hannahhoneywill.co.uk

Liam Worth is an artist working on the boundaries of material simulation, fractal geometry and ephemerality relying on a methodological mixture of 'minimal-maximal' structures. Before the artwork takes (physical) shape, his ontological approach is minutely documented in detail within a leather moleskin sketchbook. Worth's sculptures have been exhibited in London, Ascot, Oxford and Birmingham. Liam holds a first degree from Oxford Brookes, and an MA (Distinction) in Fine Art at the Birmingham Institute for Art & Design, BCU. www.cfar-biad.co.uk/liamworth

ZĒTĒSIS VOL 1. NO. 1

Journal for the Intersecting Landscapes of Fine Art,
Philosophy and the Wild Sciences.

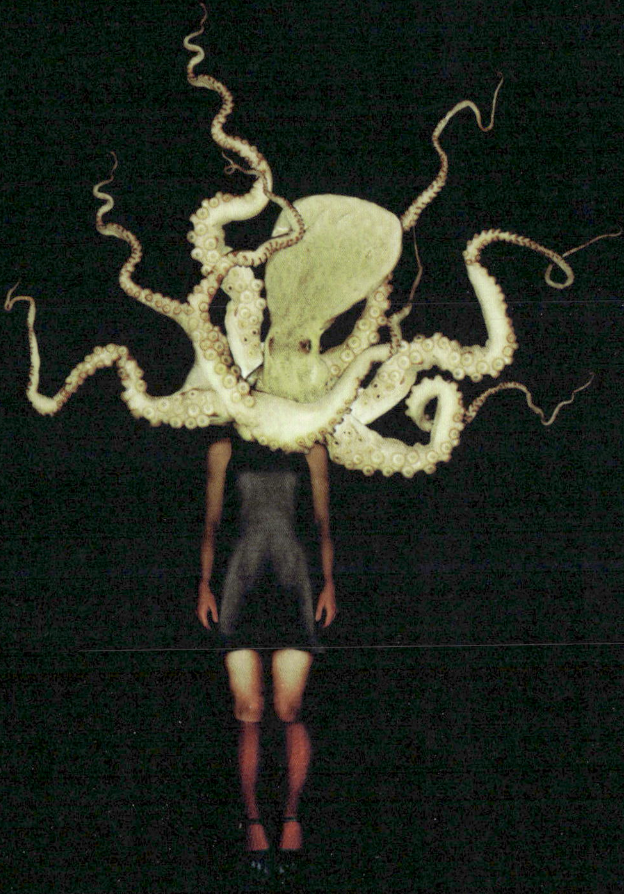

The Centre for Fine Art Research
BIRMINGHAM CITY University
ARTicle Press